MASTER YOUR VOICE

For my dad, who never lived to hear me sing with my full voice.
For my mom, who has always been my biggest fan and supporter and believed in me.
For my daughter, who is my light and joy in life and the biggest driver of why I do anything I do.
For all the dreamers out there who dare to dream BIG and follow their passion.

TABLE OF CONTENT

INTRODUCTION

Every artist has a very unique story. Since no human being is the same as any other, there are infinite ways anyone life could turn out and endless ways of how someone got where they are now. This is the wonder of life - you just can't predict an outcome by looking at a single action someone takes. Instead, a chain of countless decisions and actions is what determines the outcome.

As for me, I knew early in my life that I had an extraordinary sense for art and diving very deep in thoughts and emotions. When I compared myself to others, I saw that I was just different. I was very introverted. When I listened to classical music, I could not simply listen to it, but in my head, a movie began to unfold. I saw an emotional and compelling scene right in front of me, with characters who dramatically were entangled in life-and-death situations, deep love, melancholy, or skipping along a summer meadow with butterflies all around them. It was like the movie beamed me into another time and space. I could describe every detail of the scene because I literally lived through it.

In reverse, whenever I was sad or happy, I would start singing songs that reflected what I was feeling. And I was always someone who had a myriad of emotions, from the highest highs to the lowest lows. Since growing up in my family was often dramatic, music and art was always an outlet for my emotions and dreams. I could create a world that made me feel better when I found myself in the midst of despair or one that gave me permission to feel what I felt.

There was a lot of trauma as my dad struggled with alcohol and became very angry when he was drunk. It was a constant up and down, a daily rollercoaster since my dad was emotionally abusive when he drank but a wonderful and loving father when he was sober.

What helped me through all of this was diving deep into music and art, and I always knew I was different than most other kids since I had the longing to understand everything that was going on in life in a profound and introverted way. I was deeply in touch with my own feelings and was always highly empathic towards others and what was happening around me. I was interested not only in the arts such as classical music, opera, ballet, painting and sculpting, but also in philosophy, psychology, astrophysics, biology, and other sciences. My dad would sit down with me and explain the big bang theory, how the inner ear and the brain work, and that philosophers all essentially try to explain the meaning of life. He explained Schopenhauer, Nietzsche, Kant, Aristotle, and Marcus Aurelius to me. He always made me understand that expanding my horizons is the element that could set me apart from others and determine whether I would serve others or others would serve me in life.

And that all the hard work I would put into learning would benefit me for the rest of my life. I was taught that school was for me, that I had to study not for my teachers or parents, but for myself so I would have all the options open to me in my life.

That upbringing left a deep imprint on me and began to shape a lot of my decisions in the future because I always understood the value of investing in myself. All material things pass away, but my experiences, memories and everything I've learned will become part of who I am and potentially make my life better. I'm constantly on a mission to make myself better.

7

Freya Casey

I knew that if I wanted to become the master of something, I would have to invest a lot of time and effort into it. Nothing substantial comes easily or quickly, although music was always easy for me to understand. Understanding and doing are two completely different things.

But anytime I got into a new endeavor, whether it was ballet, horseback riding, or playing the flute, my parents supported me one hundred percent and opened up a whole world of opportunities for me. I had the best teachers, most intensive one-on-one training, went all in and wasn't allowed to skip a lesson just because I didn't feel like going. After I decided to start something, I was expected to stick with it for a while. I think this taught me early on to persevere and to work through the ups and downs that are naturally part of the learning process. I just wasn't allowed to dabble. Clearly, I also had to set priorities.

I remember the time after I had a horseback riding accident with a big horse. After several years of competitions in both dressage and jumping, this really gave my whole family a big scare, since I could have been killed. I had wanted to become a professional horse trainer and had spent ten years of my life doing almost nothing else but riding and taking care of my horses, but after the accident, we all agreed that maybe I should shift my focus onto something else. This accident really changed our thinking a lot, and we decided to sell the horse that had always been very nervous and dangerous.

Since the incident really had scared me to the bone, I was happy to choose music as a substitute, and the flute became my new hobby. My grandmother bought an excellent instrument for me after I'd had my first trial lesson and had decided that this was what I wanted to do. I was very blessed to have an excellent teacher who was very engaged and motivating, and who really had high expectations so my full potential could surface. He exposed me to 20th-century classical music, which in the beginning sounded strange to me. Nothing atonal, but I just wasn't accustomed to these sounds. He really helped me understand so many musical concepts and was convinced that I was unusually musically talented. He always gave me opportunities to perform, even making a little money on the side at small gigs, like playing in churches and small concerts. Within one year, I became so good at playing the flute that I dared to audition at the Frankfurt Music Conservatory (Hoch'sches Konservatorium) and was admitted to preparing for music university.

I remember the day of my audition: it felt so magical as I walked the halls of the building with music coming from every direction: violins, oboes, pianos, percussion, and voices. As I walked down the halls, I saw the young musicians pass me with their instruments or sheet music. I could see that music was their life. I also saw ballet dancers walking by me, and I loved how they walked with turned-out feet. They looked so graceful. The thought that I could be among all those students to become excellent at my art was so exciting.

For my audition, there were three members of the faculty in the jury. I was nervous but also confident in my skills. I had practiced the pieces I performed a lot, and all went well. Just a few days later we got the letter in the mail that I was accepted into the conservatory.

I had a great teacher, but she didn't really suit me well. It wasn't as much fun as it had been with my first teacher. All my new teacher ever did with me was technique, playing scales and solo pieces without accompaniment, whereas my former teacher had always chosen pieces I absolutely loved, and he always had accompanied me on the piano or played a duet for two flues with me. Suddenly, it wasn't about passion anymore, but just about technique, which undoubtedly is essential, but it's not the only aspect of music. Music was a matter of the heart to me. So, after one year, I left the conservatory and went back to my old teacher. And I loved it - again. He just had the gift to make everything so interesting by opening up a whole new musical world to me with every new piece of music he introduced me to. He also would always play a new piece he had for me so I could hear how awesome he played and how great it could sound. It was very inspiring.

While there probably are a lot of great teachers out there who may not be the greatest artists, they may be the very best teachers, because they really understand music and how to inspire someone to strive for excellence. They really know their stuff, and for me, there was never anything more inspiring than watching and listening to someone who is genuinely passionate. If that teacher is also a great performer, it amplifies everything tenfold. It motivates me so much to practice more after I listen to a great artist so I can learn to be more like them. Not in a way that I would want to copy them, but just in the level of skill and passion.

I always had an interest in language and paid close attention to those subtle nuances of articulation and diction in different dialects and languages. Even before I ever learned English, I pretended to speak the language by just making up words that sounded like that sound I had heard in English songs. My mom and I often acted silly and imitated different German dialects, for instance, Bavarian, Saxon, Swabian, and Northern German. I had fun imitating all sorts of sounds with my voice, anything interesting I heard and thought I could try to sound like, from a kitten's meow to an opera singer's high pitch to cartoon characters.

I actually had a lot of fun making people believe there was a real kitten or dog around somewhere, sounding as authentic as I could. I imitated dark voices, bright voices, spoken and sung, and loved to find out what parts of my throat I had to move to achieve the sound I had in mind. I figured out early on that I could move different parts of my mouth and throat to create those sounds, like the larynx, the tongue, and the soft palate. Of course, I didn't know the names for those parts yet, but I had a pretty good idea of how things worked in the voice and what made the tone change in what way.

I guess that's all because I was exposed to a lot of different music and voices and found it fascinating to listen to all kinds of different singers like opera singers, chanson singers, folk singers, and professionals in the studio. As a professional singer, my dad was often recording at a studio, and he would usually take me along. I sat through composition and recording sessions, witnessing some of the arguments and discussions that went on between the composer, the arranger, the producer, and the singer. I had a strong opinion early on whether a singer was good or awful. There were some wannabes, I remember very vividly, who said they were professional singers, but when I heard them sing I thought they were terrible. I couldn't describe exactly what I didn't like yet, but a wobbly vibrato and a lack of pitch accuracy just bothered me. I had very sensitive ears when it came to accuracy in music, both in pitch and rhythm.

In this book, I want to spark your interest to begin listening differently, to start being more interested in the nuances of sounds the human voice can create, and is continually experimenting with your own voice to find out how all the parts work. I literally want you to become a true nerd when it comes to the vocal mechanism, and begin loving the process of molding and shaping your voice. I want you to become fascinated with the emotions your voice can evoke in others, by the many colors and what happens in your voice and body when you feel happiness, sadness, despair, anger, or frustration. I want you to have an insatiable hunger to find out why certain things feel easy in your voice while other things you do put strain on your vocal cords, and why in one song you experience absolute ease while in another song you can't get that transition for the life of you, and why you go flat or sharp in certain situations.

You see, for everything that could potentially go wrong - or maybe it doesn't even have to go wrong - but for every sound that you dislike in your voice, there's a cause and a fix to change that sound to your liking. It's just a matter of understanding and getting really good at using your toolbox to shape any sound you wish to make. If you do that, you can become the sculptor of your voice, and the more skilled you become at using your sculpting tools, the more beautiful sculptures you can create, and people will admire the pieces of art you create.

For me, it was never relevant how many people got to hear my voice, but every single person - even if it was just one - who came up to me with tears in their eyes telling me how deeply they were touched by my voice, made my day and motivated me to continue and to become better every day. You see, if you can only create one short magic moment for somebody who may be going through a rough day or difficult time in their life, you've already made the world a better place by speaking through the language of music and voice, which transcends all boundaries and unites us as humans at a very profound level.

WHAT'S YOUR WHY?

You know you love to sing and that singing is a big part of your life. You have determined that you want to make the most of your skill and take it as far as you can possibly take it. You may dream of being on stage, adored and admired by your fans. You may even dream of making big money with a number one hit album.

Or, you may dream of having more confidence when you sing with others, or singing more accurately in your choir. There's just something about singing that goes beyond just knowing how to carry a tune. It's very personal and can either boost the confidence of those who know they can sing well or cause a lot of anxiety and embarrassment for those who know or THINK they can't. If you've ever been told that you sing off pitch, chances are that you simply stopped singing for years to come.

No one can tell you what dreams are too big or too small. No one can tell you what you can or cannot do. Essentially, your dreams are yours, and I'm all for dreaming big and having a growth mindset. I believe that anything is possible if you put your mind to it and work hard and consistently. There have been many who came before you who seemed to have the most unrealistic dreams, such as making human beings fly in a machine, or making light with electricity in a glass bulb. These visionaries were laughed at and ridiculed, and they failed endless times before having their breakthrough. We usually only hear about the success stories, and it almost seems like there was nothing that came before that. The truth is that there is usually a lot of pain, failure, and emotional stress that precedes the big headline stories we have come to know. What we don't see are the many years of financial struggles, the emotional strain, relationships suffering, endless sleepless nights and years of 100-hour work-weeks, the ridicule. But what would our world be like nowadays without those visionaries who believed in the unrealistic? There would be no electricity, no cars, no airplanes, no Beethoven's Fifth Symphony, no Bob Dylan songs, no Jerry Lewis movies, no smartphones, no computers, no flying across the Atlantic Ocean in a few short hours. We would probably still believe that the earth is a disc and wouldn't dare to travel too far in fear of falling off.

Do you have a vision? Do you see a clear picture of what your dreams will look like when they become a reality? Do you daydream about using your voice for something special, singing music that you love and that you send out into the world like a ship across the ocean, so that it can connect to other fellow humans and work in them? Do you feel the power your voice has when you're in tune with what's in the sound of the music as well as in your heart? Do you have a sense of the effect your voice could have on someone? Isn't it through our voices that we communicate our joy, fear, frustration, hope, and love?

I feel like everyone who has a voice has a mission to use it for something good. Whether it's calming down your child, shouting out to a stranger who's about to run into a car and thus saving his life, or connecting in a very special way in song. Humans have always sung, and every child just begins to sing naturally. It's part of who we are as humans.

Sadly enough, there's too many of us who have been told that we sound terrible or don't do it right. And so, tragically, their singing voices are muted and they don't dare to sing out anymore, which often times causes a lot of pain, because naturally we just want to sing because we express ourselves in music.

Singing is an essential part of being human, and I want you to give yourself permission right here and now to just raise your voice and never be embarrassed about any sound that comes out of your mouth. It's not about perfection, but about authenticity. It's time we begin to sing for joy once again. With joy comes passion, and with passion comes an automatic strive for improvement, which will eventually lead to excellence.

However, I also want you to know the reality of becoming a dedicated singer who strives for excellence, whether it's becoming a professional or an ambitious hobby singer. Excellence has a price. To achieve true mastery, you must invest time, your whole heart, be gritty, and never give up. You have to be ready to fail, to face setbacks, stay motivated when you plateau. You will need to learn to FOCUS: Follow One Course Until Success. There will not just be moments of success, joy, and flow, and your life will not only consist of singing and creating music, as you may already have guessed. Sometimes it will seem like all your hard work isn't paying off and that you even digress instead of progressing. Every singer whom you've ever admired walked a long path to put together that amazing show. Singing is hard work, both physically and mentally. It's unbelievably draining and you're often at the end of what you can possibly give after a great performance. But it's also the most rewarding thing you can ever do. When you know you've given everything, touched someone's life, delivered something precious and invaluable to your audience.

I just want you to know that even when you're successful, it's not all glamour and beautiful clothes, but about being absolutely and wholly in love with the art of singing and the daily path you walk to become better all the time - for your audience and for yourself.

Being a performer is physically and mentally exhausting at times. Giving your all on stage, in the studio, and in rehearsal requires you to live through intense emotions and not be afraid to physically expand all the energy you have to give. Singing is not only an art, but also a craft, and it's very physical. I often feel very exhausted after a performance. Not in a negative way, but in a sense of having nothing left I can possibly give. I'm empty and tired. In a very positive way. Singing is hard work but also lifts you incredibly high.

When I have a gig without my fellow musicians, I have to load up my heavy equipment myself, such as my digital piano, mic stands, cables, speakers, and my mixer case. I load and unload my car, haul it to wherever I will be performing at the venue. I then have to carry it inside, set it up, hook up all the cables, take everything down after the gig, load it back into my car, and unload it again when I'm back home. In the summer, all of this happens in blazing hot weather, and in the winter at freezing cold temperatures.

Sometimes there's not a room to change clothes at the venue, for example when I perform in the courtyard of a castle, at an old medieval church, or at a lakeshore, so I will have to change clothes in my car and freshen up my makeup there, too. Life as a performing artist is all about improvising, on stage and off.

Occasionally, there are those gigs which have a strange vibe. I don't feel very connected to or appreciated by the audience at all, but I can't let this get to me and start doubting myself. I still need to be unbiased and give all I've got. I may be doing that exact same performance at the same high level in two different places with two different audiences, and the reaction may vary drastically. Learning not to doubt yourself and just deliver without overthinking is a lifelong process. Sometimes, the audience is very engaged and reactive, and at other times it's exactly the opposite, no matter how much I try to connect and engage. It depends on the venue, the ambiance, even the weather, so some factors you just can't control as a performing artist.

I've been performing at a very well-known and fancy hotel with a good friend and pianist for more than ten years regularly. We play in the hotel bar, where there's also a dance floor for guests to dance. There are times when a lot of guests dance and acknowledge our music by applauding. I think we've consistently delivered first class music. However, there have been instances when no one applauded all evening long, even though I sang really demanding repertoire with a high degree of virtuosity and literally sang my heart and soul out.

Although we don't exactly appreciate those days, we just see it as part of our job that there will be times when your audience's mind is not quite on what we do, but rather in the conversations they are having with their wife, husband, children, and friends. It's wonderful to know that we provide a pleasant backdrop to their happy conversations. It's actually a compliment when people let us know that they can still carry on a conversation while we play and sing. It shows us that what we do is pleasant and appreciated instead of disturbing. I've learned that I shouldn't take a lack of audience engagement personally, and the lack of applause in some settings doesn't necessarily indicate a lack of appreciation. Having been on the other side, sitting in the audience, I always do applaud when there's live music, but when I'm in a bar or restaurant, my focus definitely is more on the conversation I'm having with the person I'm spending the evening with. Putting yourself in the shoes of the audience can really help you be more confident and diminish doubt in your skills as a singer. If anything, you can always learn from a performance that didn't go as you had anticipated.

As a matter of fact, „Improvise" should become your middle name if you desire to become a performing artist. Something unexpected will always happen, whether it's your voice cracking on that high pitch that you always nailed in rehearsals, the mic cutting out on you, or the pianist messing up the entrance.

Fortunately, these instances of not feeling fully appreciated for the effort are not the norm and rather rare. But they do exist. The many positive remarks and comments that you will have coming your way more than make up for this. You just have to learn to get into the mindset of not doubting you skills and artistry just because your audience isn't reacting exactly the way you had imagined.

To build your repertoire, you will need to focus and work for months and even years with lots of rehearsals and practice sessions. It took me many years to acquire the vast repertoire I have today. If I added up all of the pieces I know in opera, art song, oratorio, chanson, pop, gospel, soul, jazz, folk, klezmer, rock, Schlager, country, blues, and swing, I could probably perform twenty four hours a day for a whole week without running out of new songs. I learn new songs all the time, while doing new projects and studying songs with my students they love which are new to me, but there's still so much repertoire I have never even heard. The vastness of music in this world is literally infinite. Even within one genre, just when you think you know a lot, there are still so many songs you've never heard of. I love digging out those gems that aren't widely performed, but I know I will wow my audience because of their beauty. Being open to new sounds and experiments will make you a better singer. Having fun tweaking your voice, trying different ways of phrasing, and working out the angle you want to take is essential. Besides always working on your technique, you must develop an edge that makes you unique. You have something special. If you don't know yet what it is, you must find out.

I actually love performing by myself, because it reduces rehearsal time. Whenever there are other musicians involved, it takes time and communication to work out the arrangements and timings, transitions, dynamic levels, and the underlying feeling you want to communicate. The more musicians are involved, the longer it will take to get it all tight. Everyone has their own opinion and taste. I've worked with many world-class professional musicians, and even though each and everyone is awesome at what they do, playing together is a whole different story. There are musicians I just click with and others which feel music entirely differently, and it's a lot harder to work with those.

When I met my pianist who is now one of my best friends, I immediately felt a connection. He felt music in a very similar way that I did. We basically didn't have to talk a lot, because he understood what I did with my voice and followed me. He is an excellent listener, and I'm also a very sensitive listener. Because our personalities are similar in so many ways, we express music very similarly.

On the other hand, I've had to work with some musicians that made me feel totally lost and disconnected. They didn't get at all what I wanted to express and just had a whole different sentiment. It just didn't work. Well, basically the audience heard all the correct pitches, and everything was at a really high level of performance skill, but there's just a whole other level you can get to when you really gel as a performing team. You need to become one, not competing with one another, but listening carefully to every intricate detail and always setting the stage for the singer, who has words to communicate.

By the way, there's no such thing as enough rehearsal time. So often, I have to perform with an orchestra after only a single short rehearsal just to establish tempi and transitions. This short rehearsal usually takes place right before the concert begins. So, whatever changes or directions the conductor suggests to me, I have to remember right then and there. This is when it's important to make notes and go over these in a quiet moment to internalize them. You must always carry a pencil or be able to make notes on your tablet (I always use my iPad for my sheet music). Over time, I've learned to improvise on the spot if something doesn't quite go according to plan, and that happens more often than you may think. As a singer, you have to train your brain to literally work on multiple levels simultaneously: shaping words, acting, listening to the band or orchestra, watching a conductor, and connecting with your audience, all while singing accurately and having good posture and support throughout. As you can imagine, this can only happen with a lot of practice, since these processes become more and more automatic the more you practice them. You have to literally rewire your brain to be creative on the spot, to do something when something unexpected happens. It may be something in your voice placement that goes awry, it may be that you forgot the lyrics, or the orchestra may be jumping ahead a couple of measures suddenly, being way too slow or way too fast. I've had conductors who totally got the tempo wrong even after we had agreed on it. We're all only human, so mistakes do happen. A good performing artist isn't scared of something unexpected happening, but actually has fun when it happens.

And then there are sound technicians. They can be your greatest curse or your greatest blessing. At big concerts with professional sound technicians and PA system at the venue, you will be completely at the mercy of the sound engineer and equipment. There are really great ones who will gladly make some changes to help you out, such as turning up your monitors, adding more high frequencies or a little more reverb. However, I have encountered quite a few who just didn't have a good musical ear. They simply didn't know how to mix right and make it sound great. In the end, you're in the spotlight. Make sure you communicate what you want and need. Once, a sound technician suggested I should sing "My Heart Will Go On" from the movie Titanic without any reverb, completely dry. It sounded so dead and had no space. I thought he was kidding me. Despite his opinion, I kindly asked him to put reverb on my vocals, so he did. We had to tweak it a bit because he didn't really have a sense for how much was enough and how much was too much. It's important that the sound you hear reflects your taste since otherwise, you will subconsciously try to adjust your voice and technique, which is bad because it will strain your voice. When you can't hear yourself, you will yell into the mic, trying to compensate. When you hear yourself too loud, you will try to sing softer, which can be really hard and straining on high belted pitches.

As a successful performing artist, you will most likely travel quite a bit. By car, by train, by airplane… you will usually spend more time traveling than performing. I have traveled across the country just to sing three songs for a big concert. So you have to train yourself to give one hundred percent on demand even if you've had a long day traveling since you will only have one chance when you sing a single song during a concert. This is why a well established warm-up routine is an absolute MUST. Know your voice and your body, any foods or drinks you may react to that cause phlegm or dryness, and get into the habit of practicing meditation to keep you calm when things get hectic, which they definitely do at times. Take care of your body, because your body is your instrument. Being physically fit is definitely a plus and will help you have more endurance as well as clarity of mind.

There's also something to be said about the time you need to invest in work that has absolutely nothing to do with singing or music. You want to perform, right? If you don't have an agent - and I've always preferred to be independent and have control over every part of the process - you will need to exchange a lot of emails with people who ask for rates or those who have already booked you. You have to make phone calls, coordinate times, decide what repertoire to sing, and when and how much to charge.

Even as an ambitious hobby singer, you have to manage your projects, organize your sheet music, communicate with organizers, choir directors, conductors, and lots of other people involved in the event.

If you're not very organized, you may prepare the wrong songs, get the starting time of the gig or rehearsal dates wrong, or show up to the wrong location. You need to be your own very organized secretary. I've established systems over the years that make everything smoother and help me stay in control. But still, I have to admit that I've accidentally had some double bookings. Once you've established yourself by having delivered great performances, you will begin to get more emails and phone calls asking you to perform again. Someone may call you up out of the blue asking if you're free to perform at their event. You should know the answers ahead of time. Otherwise, you will blurt out something you may regret later. You should know what you want to charge early on, because if people like what you do they will want you to come and provide music for their event, too. I remember many years ago making up my rates on the spot as I was talking on the phone to someone who wanted to book me, hoping it wouldn't be too much since I really needed the money. It's not good to be insecure about your rates. Know your worth and stick to it. If someone doesn't want to pay your rates, they obviously don't see your value, and you wouldn't want to perform for them anyway. Once I got to a place of not needing all the gigs I get requested for, I also got more secure just naming my price with confidence, which definitely helps with getting booked. There's just something about radiating confidence in your skills that draws people to you. That is, of course, if you really do have the skills.

A task that I actually hate (and I have no idea why) is sending bills. It is an essential task though, and you need to be on top of it at all times. I'm an artist and hate office work. I'd rather just show up for the performance. But I need to get paid. The shady side of this is that there, unfortunately, could be instances when you don't get paid or have to wait for your money for way too long. I've had this happen a few times. The agency that hired me actually went bankrupt shortly after my performance, so I didn't get to see any money. The really annoying part is that I had quite a bit of expense for travel and equipment that I had forked out. Another time I sang for a wedding, the lady who booked me - which wasn't the bride but a friend of hers - had forgotten to bring the envelope with the money. Well, I never saw my money even after months of chasing after her via email and phone.

Another task that I found difficult at the beginning of my career was picking out clothes for my performances. While it is fun to shop for beautiful evening gowns, the process of selecting a professional stage outfit needs to be done very carefully and consciously. It's not about picking what you like, but what looks good on you on stage, what represents your personality and style, suits the musical style, and works with stage lighting. Certain patterns don't work on stage or camera, and also some asymmetrical shapes can make your body look awkward from a distance. You also need to keep in mind that you will have to breathe in your clothes, meaning you have to make sure they're not too tight when you fully inhale. I suggest taking a deep breath as if you were getting ready to sing when you try on a stage outfit. You also shouldn't pick clothes that don't stay put. For instance, if there's a strap that keeps sliding down your shoulder or a skirt that keeps riding up your legs, it will distract you from your performance, as you are constantly conscious of it and try to fix it. So when you try on your outfit, move around a bit, bend over, lift your arms, sit and walk to make sure it will allow you to do your work on stage.

When I was performing some opera arias in a concert in Italy, my zipper broke just as someone helped me zip up the back right before I had to get onto the stage. I had to go out on stage with an open zipper. As I was stepping onto the stage, I pressed my arms tightly against the sides of my body so I wouldn't lose the dress. It was awkward and really distracting for me. I did very well as far as the singing was concerned, but I couldn't really perform well since I couldn't move my arms. I tried to emote as well as I could with my hands and the lower part of my arms, but I'm sure it looked a little weird. Since then, I always bring a spare dress to every gig. By the way, the zipper problem has since happened again more than once.

When you pick shoes, they should not keep you from moving

around naturally. You shouldn't wear shoes with extremely high heels if you have never worn shoes like that before. You just don't want your outfit, shoes, or jewelry to take your attention away from your actual performance. Even your hairdo can be distracting when you find a strand of hair repeatedly falling into your face and keep throwing it back as you sing.

I also address these issues in my video course "Conquer Your Stage Fright", which you can find at www.masteryourvoice.tv. Anything that distracts you takes away from your confidence.

Don't underestimate how much work it is to get your clothes to and from your gig. I've had concerts, in which I wore seven different dresses, some of them very heavy with pannier, and I literally had to do a heavy workout just hauling them from my car into the dressing room. Nowadays, I have a whole closet full of clothes that are only for the stage, so it's a good thing I never changed my clothes size during my adult life. If I had to rebuy everything, it would cost me a fortune, as some of the dresses were quite pricey. Building your stage wardrobe may take years, but you will find you have go-to pieces you keep coming back to and that you love most. You simply can't know how well an outfit will work before you've actually worn it for a whole performance. So, try to keep your dress size.

The reason why I'm telling you all of this is that I want you to know what to expect. Being a performing artist is a lot of work, so you better make sure you love it enough to where you are ready to deal with all of these not-so-glamorous tasks. If you're truly passionate, no task will be too hard.

If I asked you why you want to be a singer, you should know the answer. What is your why? Is it because you can't imagine doing anything else and would give up almost anything to do what you love? Would you be willing to spend years without making vast amounts of money, singing at small venues? Is money secondary, because you have such a strong desire to make people happy with your music and love to give a piece of yourself? Have you tried other jobs and found yourself singing and writing songs the whole time? Do you suffer when you don't get to sing and share your music with people?

If your answer to any or all of these questions is "yes", you may indeed be on the right track to becoming a successful singer. Always keep in mind that your audience can expose someone inauthentic and fake easily. So you better make sure it's not about being cool, admired, or money, but about genuinely loving what you do no matter the cost. Only when you are willing to exhaust yourself and give it your all, can you become a world-class singer.

World-class also means giving to the world. And the beautiful thing we do as performing artists is that we create lovely moments in time, experiences, dreams, escapes, wishes - all these wonderful things that may not be tangible and measurable, but are so valuable in a human's life. We have the opportunity to give a piece of our heart and receive gratitude in return.

Of course, we also need to allow people to show us their appreciation us by paying us. But this shouldn't be the primary objective. Our job goes way beyond just performing tasks, finishing at a particular time, being done, and going home. What we do is an integral part of our lives, and our lives are mirrored in the way we perform. We essentially tell our own stories when we're on stage, we expose our pain points, struggles, hopes, and dreams. It's very personal. I don't think there's a job that could be more personal than being a singer. You have to give a big piece of yourself, and yet find a way to balance that with your daily personal and family life.

Your why has to be strong enough to withstand rejection, disappointments, discouragement, financial hardships, and adversity. Not everybody will love what you do, so it takes a lot of confidence in yourself and your skills. Doubts will creep in from time to time, but you need to know that will continue no matter what.

If you are ready to continue learning, to never stand still, to always be hungry for new sounds and experiments, you may really be prepared to get serious about becoming a world class singer.

HOW TO BECOME A MASTER

I believe we all can agree on the fact that everyone has a different definition of a world class singer. I've experienced it over and over again that someone told me about a singer he or she was absolutely crazy about and they just couldn't stop listening to their voice because it was the most impressive sound, almost out of this world. With high expectations and full of hope, I went to find some recordings or videos, but as the first few measures began to play, I was utterly disappointed: it's alright, I thought. But I had expected so much more. It just didn't resemble the description my friend had given.

The same happened the other way around when I was head over heels for a song that I thought resembled nothing less than music created by angels. But to my disappointment, my friend's casual remark was only: it's ok...

What?! How can you possibly not be moved to tears by that song, those rich and lush harmonies, those ingenious melody lines? You must be from another planet!

Well, it only shows that music is very much a matter of taste, and everyone will fancy different sounds.

It's just a fact of life that each and every person is different and simply has a different taste. And it does not really have anything to do with how musically educated someone is. My best friend and pianist, who is a very accomplished professional musician, loves songs that are very simplistic, even minimalistic, and listens to music that I find very dull and repetitive. However, he still appreciates and loves some the same music I love. And some of what I love, he doesn't love so much. We still click when it comes to feeling and performing the music we play and sing together.

The biggest lesson I've learned as a performing artist who has been on stage for decades is that I can't possibly please everyone by the mere sounds I produce, i.e., the timbre of my voice. Some will love it, some won't. But what I CAN do to convince even the toughest critic is to go deeper than just singing with great technique and outstanding musicality. The moment I add my heart and soul to my performance, live through the music and words as if my life depended on it, give everything and exhaust myself in the process of just connecting to my most vulnerable and human essence of who I am, something magical happens: hearts soften and open up, and I can feel my audience connect with me and live through every nuance of what I'm experiencing. Every emotion I feel, every gesture I make, every vibe I send out, comes back full circle, and this crazy thing happens: we all forget where we are and what time it is, we just connect as human beings.

Little mistakes are no longer mistakes - they show that I'm human and not perfect. My audience doesn't crave absolute perfection. While they do want me to sing on pitch (I mean: who wants to ever listen to a singer who sings off pitch?), they want me to have ease in my voice and not hear any technical struggles. And that's the true art of being a world-class singer: melting into the music in a way that unites technique, musicality, and the art of connecting with other human beings on a deeper level. Once you get to a point where your virtuosity and technique becomes automatic, you can focus on truly connecting with the music and your audience.

Did you notice that the title of the book is "Master Your Voice" - not "Become A World Famous Singer"? Do you really want to be world famous? Do you want to be in the media?

Do you want to sacrifice your personal life? Do you necessarily need to have a contract with a record label? Do you have to be known by everyone? Personally, the biggest asset I've always valued in my life was freedom. That's the main reason why I've never had an agent or a label, although it has been recommended by some professionals I've worked with. I just wouldn't want to give up the luxury of doing everything I do on my own terms, of deciding what music to sing, what gigs to say no to, and where to travel. How to move on stage, how many songs to sing. I have complete freedom to decide where to appear and what people I'd rather not work with.

Sure, scheduling gigs and planning everything out may present a big task and mean more work when you do it all without outsourcing, but believe me - I would never trade being one hundred percent my own boss for anything in the world.

Besides, in today's world, you can actually have freedom and success. You can self publish books (just like I did with this one), sell your songs on iTunes, Amazon, and Spotify, make money from YouTube, online courses and lessons. There are musicians like Boyce Avenue, Max Schneider, and Kurt Hugo Schneider who are very successful in marketing themselves via YouTube. Not only do they generate income from the views, but they also go on tours filling big halls.

In today's fast-paced and impersonal world everybody longs for a human connection, for intimacy, for genuine encounters with real people, for vulnerability. We are all attracted to people around whom we can let our guards down, who make us feel connected and understood. The truth is, that hidden behind our hectic and complicated lives are just very fragile personalities who crave the simple things in life: happiness, love, safety, belonging, peace. It's what we essentially all long for. It's what's left when you strip everything else away, our daily hustle and bustle, without overthinking or overcomplicating life. It's what every child intuitively is drawn to: real and honest human connection. Authenticity. Plain and simple.

And this is precisely what you should never forget if you genuinely want to become a world-class singer: how to combine your vocal virtuosity and musicality with deep emotions, your own authentic story, and genuine personality. Besides the prerequisite of singing in tune (which you should always be obsessed about perfecting), you have to become the world's best storyteller and psychologist. You have to get into your audience's mind by connecting on a profound level. You have to open up to the necessity of exposing your own imperfection. That's what is so hard for a lot of singers.

Of course, you want to improve your technique and have perfect intonation. But believe me: if I had to choose between a robot singing pitch perfect and a human being who put all of their heart, sweat and tears into their performance but sang their song just a little bit off pitch here and there: I would choose the slightly off pitch human any day over a robot that apparently doesn't sing about anything he has experienced.

Unfortunately, there are way too many singers who are missing the critical element. I remember countless times when I went to concerts and the singer was basically great in regards to their technique. While the concert progressed, everything seemed so amazing and perfect. But something was missing, they didn't really connect. It was like there was a wall between them and me. I couldn't feel that they gave all of their heart, that they laid it all at my feet. You know what happened after the concert? It just didn't stick! I forgot the performance pretty quickly because there wasn't an intense feeling the singer evoked in me.

We know that our most vivid memories come from experiences that cut deeply into our minds. Not only traumatic events such as a death in the family, but also happy instances like the birth of a baby or a marriage proposal, or an experience in a place that was incredibly amazing, like standing on the peak of a mountain or seeing the ocean for the first time. We engrave those moments deep into our memories, it's like time stands still for a moment and we take a still shot of our life at that exact moment. We remember so many details, but what we really remember most is how we felt and how the world looked to us at that moment.

You have to learn to allow yourself to show your feelings, share your most intimate stories, and be vulnerable. Everyone has a soft spot, a place of vulnerability. When we try to hide it, we come across as inauthentic. You're already what you need to be - just be more of who you already are and be proud of being you.

CAN YOU BECOME A WORLD CLASS SINGER?

If you are reading this book, you must believe that you can eventually become a world-class singer. Or, at least you think there's the possibility to improve. Or, maybe you are not convinced, but you wish you could actually turn yourself into a great singer one day that has the confidence to perform in front of an audience who adores you as an artist, and you are just reading this book because the title challenged you.

I'm here today to tell you that you CAN become a world-class singer if you are ready to put in the work it takes, change your mindset, have lots and lots of patience, the willingness to battle your doubts and fears, and trust your instincts. You can become an artist that captivates your audience, and whose songs move others to tears because they touch on a very deep and profound level. You can be that singer-songwriter who just needs a guitar and voice to draw people in. You just haven't found your identity yet, your message, a way to communicate your authentic personality, and a healthy vocal technique that will allow you to do all of this.

Once you have these prerequisites, there are virtually no limits as to what you can achieve. And I want to show you what steps you need to take to begin your journey to become a world-class singer and change the world a little bit at a time with all the goodness you have to give.

The first questions you need to ask yourself are: what do I have that no other artist has? What is unique about me? What are my quirks that distinguish me from other singers? What are my strengths and what weaknesses do I need to work on?

I know that those are huge questions that aren't easy to answer. This may take some deep digging, but unless you know the answers, you will not become an outstanding artist. You must know what your biggest assets are, since these are the things people will be drawn to and pay money for. And you must gain confidence in those strengths, because these are your selling points that will allow you to be successful.

Since it may be difficult to come up with answers, I want to help you a little by guiding you towards recognizing the essence of who you are:

Is there a very unique pain point in your life? Have there been moments of deep pain in the past (or maybe even in the present) that carved a deep wound into your heart? This may be a good clue as to what touches you personally. Your weak and soft spots will open up doors to become more real and vulnerable and to find your voice to express something that is near and dear to your heart, something that reaches deeper than anything else in your life. Maybe you lost a loved one, and this has left a void inside of your heart. Whenever you sing a song like "Tears in Heaven", you may feel a very special connection to the song, since you can't help but live through your memories each and every time you sing it. This is exactly what any singer's audience craves: someone to empathize with, someone who is telling their own story in a very undistorted and honest way, someone who allows others to see his own weaknesses without holding back any part.

Maybe you have a very cheerful and upbeat personality and are all about fun, have always been the one to cheer others up when they are upset or go through difficult times. If it comes easily to you to spread good vibrations, and you find everybody's face cheering up when you join the party, this may be something you can use to connect with your audience. Everyone has so many worries and problems these days, and in our fast-paced and often impersonal world of high pressure and expectations, everybody longs for some time-out and to be able to forget everything for a just short moment. You could be the artist who just makes people feel good with their music and energy, because you authentically radiate that positive energy we all need and crave. And you've experienced the power of a song, how it can immediately improve your mood.

Maybe you have a very unique voice color like Kate Bush, Tom Waits, Janis Joplin, Bob Dylan, Joanna Newsom, Ray Charles, or Shaggy. Maybe your strength is a beautiful but soft voice like Enya, Norah Jones, or Nick Drake. You may be a natural belter like Whitney Houston, Barbara Streisand, or Beyoncé.

You just have to be aware of what differentiates your voice from others, so that you can work on showcasing your strengths while working on improving on your weaknesses (which we all have). No matter what voice color or type you have or what makes your personality unique and special, there's something that only you possess.

Maybe your gift is to draw people in because you evoke trust and make it easy for people to approach you and open up to you. Whatever the case may be, you have to learn to let your uniqueness shine so it can make a difference in someone else's life.

You can do that by choosing repertoire that suits your voice and personality, and then sing it in a way that makes it your own. Just think of Jamie Cullum and his rendition of Rihanna's "Please Don't Stop the Music", which he sings and plays in a completely new and unique way that is his own style. He owns the song as if was created just for him. This is a great example of a singer who knows his strength and creates the sound that uses his unique strengths to create something new and interesting.

There are definitely examples of singers who have less than spectacular voices when it comes to technique or timbre, but who are great artists by other means, such as Johnny Cash, Ian Dury, Nick Cave, or Robert Smith (The Cure). While they may not have won a contest for the most beautiful voice color and virtuosity, they had a very distinct style and sound and knew how to make it their own. Of course, beauty is very much a matter of taste and can be argued about. But the result of their uniqueness is something that is definitely out of the norm. So, don't put yourself in a box and limit your possibilities, just because you think you have to sound or look a certain way.

While you may adore the voice of Ariana Grande, Beyoncé, Ed Sheeran, or Bruno Mars, you will never sound just like them, and that's a good thing. Vice versa, they also will never sound like you. Nobody can! You're truly unique. That's why it's so important for you to find your own style, know your strengths, and continue working on areas of your technique you may not have mastered yet. You just need to begin working with what you have right now and get started. The most important thing is that you do get started. Every day you waste hesitating or doubting and not taking action is a day more that separates you from getting connected to your uniqueness to where it becomes part of every performance.

I've heard so many aspiring singers tell me: „I'll do it when I have more confidence", or „I'll do it once I've mastered belting", or „I'll really get serious when I have learned more repertoire". All I can tell you is that the only thing that guarantees that you will get nowhere is you not taking any action. The best time to begin was yesterday. If you missed it, the second best time is right now!

The first step to begin finding out what makes you unique is to ask others what they love about your voice, and how they feel when they listen to you sing. If you ask ten people of different ages, they may say different things, but you will most likely find a common denominator and get an idea of what really stands out.

Apart from asking others how they perceive your voice, it's essential that you listen to yourself, which is best done by listening to recordings of yourself. There's something about a decent studio recording that makes it extremely useful: when you use a decent mic and use it correctly, you will hear every frequency, every nuance in your voice, every beautiful silvery or breathy sound, but also all of the little flaws. Your voice gets exposed, and you want to listen to your voice this closely as much as you can. This should become a routine because there is so much you learn from listening to yourself.

I personally have learned so much from listening to my studio recordings. It's different from a recording you may make with the built-in mic of your smartphone or even a recording from a live show. Singing in a studio setting makes you focus and bring out subtle variations in voice color because you focus only on your voice. You can also hear the sound of your breath and the nuanced shades of vowels and consonants so much better in a studio recording. Nowadays, you don't need to book an expensive studio with a professional sound technician to get your hands on a proper studio recording. You can set up a small home studio with a minimal investment of about 200 Dollars. All you need is an audio interface and a good mic, and of course, some cables to connect all of the pieces.

Not only will frequent recording help you get a good amount of practice singing with a mic in a studio setting, but it will also document your progress as you can listen to older recordings and hear what has changed in your way of singing. I try to make a recording at least once a year with each of my voice students. Not only is it great for tracking your singing journey and proving that the lessons actually help you to improve, but it also makes for an excellent gift for friends and family. Just burn a CD with your songs, create some beautiful cover art, and it will look like a CD you purchased on Amazon. You can also upload the tracks to platforms such as Soundcloud and Youtube to get exposure or to provide a way to send people to your recordings via a link. It's so easy nowadays to distribute your music. You must take advantage of all of these free ways to be heard by people all over the world. If you record your own songs and actually feel like the recordings have great quality, you can sell them online and begin making some money. Using platforms such as CD Baby, you can distribute your mastered recordings on iTunes, Amazon, and Spotify.

While you may not like the sound of your voice at this time, it is important to learn to love your voice. As you explore all facets of possible voice colors and learn to control your voice better, you will begin to hear the moments of „sparkle" that stand out. I'm absolutely sure that, even if you think you don't have a beautiful voice, you don't dislike it all the time. There are moments when you feel like there's a moment of beauty when it feels good and sounds great. That's what you need to build on.

What did you do that exact moment when you loved the sound? Get to the bottom of it and do more of it! And those moments when you feel it's excruciating to listen to your own voice: what exactly don't you like about it? Try to find out what precisely you do in those moments, and avoid doing it. It's all about learning and sorting out the pleasant and unpleasant sounds. And learn to give it a name. Don't just say: I sound terrible. But try to explain it, such as: I sound raspy, there's no resonance, I sound narrow and pressed. That will help you identify the problem so you can find a solution.

HOW LONG WILL IT TAKE?

Learning how to sing and be a great performing artist is not an event, it's a never-ending process. Much like learning a language, there are endless facets of what you can actually do with your voice. The human voice is the most amazing, versatile, and at the same time the most complex and somewhat mysterious of all musical instruments. You can't see what happens when you sing, you can just feel and hear it. Your psyche's role is just as important as your body's. Music and singing involves your physical body, emotions, logic, social skills, empathy, language, math, listening and matching, so both sides of your brain are working together. There are not many activities that do that.

Creating a sound or a certain pitch isn't as easy as just plucking a string or pressing down a key. You can't actually see what happens with your vocal cords, your larynx, your pharynx, soft palate, cricothyroid and glottis when you sing. Even if you knew in theory how it all works physiologically, it still doesn't mean you can actually do it. And having absolute control over your voice is really, really hard and takes a lot of practice. A lot!

In my studio, I use an approach that is a mix of understanding the physiology of singing, practical exercises to feel the different parts that move and need to be coordinated in phonation, and mental exercises to connect to the meaning of the music and lyrics and translate that into your voice color. And there are many variations of voice colors you can create. For example, when you speak in slow motion, stretching out the vowels, you will easily get a feeling for how to use your mid-range chest voice.

Master Your Voice

On the other hand, when you screech like a little girl, you will feel your high head voice engage. These are often very useful ways to connect to your voice and help you feel the subtleties of what you actually do with your voice every single day. To me, it's absolutely amazing how we all use our voices on a daily basis without even paying any attention to what we do. It has become a little bit of an obsession of mine to always want to analyze what somebody does with their voice even when speaking. Especially when there's something weird going on, like an incorrect vowel or consonant placement, breathiness, or lowered larynx.

Sometimes I notice a radio announcer speaking with a very low soft palate, which results in a very nasal and shallow sound. At times, I hear a singer shape the consonant "s" in a weird way. For example, when Mariah Carey sings an „s", her somewhat mispronounced "s" will stick out to where I can't focus on anything else. I absolutely love her as a singer, but that's just something I notice and after a while it begins to sound funny.

I can't help but notice when someone lowers the larynx to create a thicker sound on high belted pitches. If you want to figure out your own voice, you have to begin listening in a whole new way. I'm amazed at how many female singers - and even vocal coaches - can't tell when someone is singing in head voice or chest voice. Yes, it is hard to hear in some singers when they transition and when they're in chest voice, head voice, or mixed voice, but if you want to take your own voice to the next level and desire to truly understand the voice and all its possibilities, you need to become an expert at those things. You have to learn how to achieve the sound you're aiming for in a healthy and sustainable way, and it's a combination of knowing, watching, imitating, exploring, and repeating over and over again until you feel what works and what doesn't.

You know that when your voice gets fatigued quickly - then it's time to over think your technique and find a different way. There are endless possibilities how to make the different parts of your voice synch. Once you develop a good sense of what is happening and how it affects the sound of the voice, you will find that it's so much fun to make a game out of it.

Already as a child, I loved imitating funny voices, even the sound of foreign languages that I didn't know. You have to become interested in those intricacies, even to the degree of obsession if you want to become a true master. You have to become hungry for exploring your voice in depth.

You may already get a notion about how long of a process perfecting your voice can be, while "perfect" could mean a lot of things and is very much a matter of taste and the genre you sing in. It will mean something different to everyone, but most importantly, your goal should be to feel ease when you sing and be happy with the sounds of your voice. It's as much mental work as it is a technical process. But if you keep that in mind and are ready for making it a life long work in progress, you will always be happy with where you are, while at the same time aiming for constant improvement. The journey is so much fun if you let it. And I can tell you that your voice will continue to change throughout your life, no matter how old or young you are or how long you have been singing. Even the biggest masters always keep on learning, improving and changing their approach. Maybe it's not so much about getting "better"as it is about evolving, much like your body keeps evolving and your voice will have to do this alongside your body and mind, because YOU are your instrument.

I will elaborate on some strategies later on in the book,

because I believe you need a battle plan in order to achieve your short term as well as your long term goals. Most importantly, I want you to have fun on the way, because as soon as you lose your motivation, you won't follow through. That's why routines to form good habits are so important. More on that later. You have to find ways to keep yourself motivated. For me, listening to great music and great singers always motivates me to practice.

To get to where I am today, I had to have a lot of patience and always believe that my voice had beauty. And I had to learn to love the sound of it.

Here's my journey in a nutshell: As a daughter of musicians, I was exposed to the world of music early on. I got to watch many great singers: in opera theater, at concerts, in the recording studio. My parents worked in these places as artists, so I was right in the middle of it. It was normal. I already had a strong opinion about what sounded good and didn't like certain singers, especially the ones who had a really wide and wobbly vibrato (you know, the kind of vibrato that makes the pitch sound like two or three pitches) and voices that sounded somehow artificial and unnatural, just fake in some way. I developed a taste for singers who could sing very clean and clear, who had excellent control and intonation. It was painful to hear someone sing slightly off pitch or with a voice color that seemed totally pressed, pushed or just overachieving.

I began playing the piano when I was 6 years old and sang along with what I played. I wrote my first little songs that reflected the way I felt, which often wasn't happy because my dad had a severe alcohol problem. I think that laid the foundation for my ears to become very sensitive.

I sang in children's choir, and it wasn't about perfect

technique rather than singing together and having fun. There were many moments of awe when everyone sang together in harmony - it felt like magic. Nobody ever told me that there was anything wrong with my singing or that my voice didn't sound right. I think that gave me a wonderful starting point, because I was always encouraged to experiment in my child-like curiosity to learn, and everyone around me - my mom, my friends, my teachers - just wanted to sing together. I know that not everyone was blessed to have this wonderful way to discover music and singing freely. For many of you, childhood may be where the struggles you now have with singing began. It's when your freedom to express yourself in your natural voice was taken, you were advised to stop singing because you were singing off pitch, and began to let your voice morph into a timid and shy remnant of what was once inside of you. But that's not really you. You began holding back to avoid criticism, became insecure because you didn't know what's right anymore, and finally just stopped singing altogether. What happened to the little child that sang with joy from the top of her lungs?

I know that everybody naturally loves to sing, because it's such a unique way to express ourselves and deal with the stress of daily life, or just to allow our joy to come out because it bubbles over. It just feels good. But when we're told that we can't sing and it sounds terrible, we start questioning ourselves and feel like there's something wrong with us if we continue. It takes a lot of confidence for someone to sing in front of other people, and that confidence is taken instantly from a child by seemingly innocent casual remarks about vocal imperfections. I urge you: if you have children, sing with them. Sing with them simply for the joy of it and because it connects you. Don't ever criticize a child's voice in a negative way, not even slightly. It may cause huge damage in their self-confidence, not just in singing, but even in speaking up in front of others.

Why is it that everybody admires singers who have strong and clear voices, who sing in front of an audience with confidence? It's not just the sound of the voice itself. There's something about a confident person who raises their voice that draws us in. When I'm asked what I do for a living, and I answer that I'm a professional singer, I usually get a reaction of awe and surprise. It's almost like I'm from another planet, since a lot of people don't view being a performing artist as a normal job. I guess there aren't as many professional singers as there are accountants or secretaries, but there seems to be something special about being a professional singer.

People have a huge amount of respect for the fact that someone gets out in front of an audience to put themselves out there to perform… and be vulnerable. Especially for someone who makes a full-time living with it. I mean, how many things could go wrong? What a risk! You could sing a wrong pitch, your voice could crack, and you may be offbeat, or just lose your voice because you're so nervous. Most people avoid taking too many risks in life, but that's exactly what has to become second nature to a performing artist. Risk-takers are most admired, and as a performer you completely put yourself out there and have to improvise and be spontaneous. Almost like someone who skydives, completes a marathon, moves to a different continent. There's just something about that. And singing is actually so much less risky, but so much more personal. When your voice fails, it's almost like there's something wrong with YOU.

You must not hold back any part of you. You have to take the risk of making a mistake in front of hundreds or thousands of people. You always have to be willing to take that risk, because you're just a human being, and even singers with the most grounded technique and most beautiful voice will have some imperfections, jumble up words, crack on that high pitch, have phlegm on their vocal cords in the middle of the song, or come in on the wrong count. There are better days than others, sometimes you're tired, sometimes wired - and it all affects your voice and performance.

Being perfect isn't the objective, but daring to risk showing your imperfections and not making a big deal out of them is your bread and butter.

You have to free yourself from all of that baggage you may still carry around from your childhood when it comes to confidence and mindset, and begin exploring every aspect of your voice, which is very much an extension of your personality.

Of course, we shouldn't forget about technique, since it is an important part of the journey and will take up a lot of your time. You absolutely must develop a healthy technique if you want to stay in the game for the long run. No matter what your goals are as a singer or what level of mastery you aim for, you must become a life long student and continue to work out those muscles that control your voice. You must develop routines and good habits, so you can strengthen your voice every day and gain better control all the time. Believe me, this never stops. I learn new things all the time, and it's fun exploring even better control, intonation, range, and voice colors - not to speak of becoming a better actor and performer that can captivate an audience.

Even after singing all of my life and studying as well as teaching voice for more than 15 years, I still learn about new approaches all the time, as I experiment and try out different techniques to achieve the sound I want in a more efficient way. Do you see how long this journey is? It never stops!

Never!

I guess that's why I don't know a single musician who ever really retired. Sure, they may not tour or record albums anymore, but not a single artist I know ever stopped singing or playing his or her instrument right until the time they physically absolutely couldn't. And the only reason not to make music would be paralysis or death.

Your progress will depend on several factors: the amount of time you spend studying and practicing, the frequency, your focus, your physical condition, your theoretical knowledge to understand the principles of how the voice works, your natural abilities, your learning style, your tenacity and commitment.

How much time should you spend practicing?

This will vary depending on your endurance, and also depends on how and what you practice. Let's say your goal is to practice high belted out pitches to increase your range on the top: since you will have to do high-intensity exercises to train your voice to get stronger, you won't be able to maintain this level of tension for a long time. In this case, it's better to practice at high intensity for just five minutes and then come back to it after doing some lower intensity exercises.

When you sing a song that's very demanding on the vocal cords, high volume, high intensity, pushing your vocal cords to their limit, you certainly can't continue singing through that song as many times as you could through a very relaxed song that sits more in the middle and low range of your voice. You have to develop a very good feeling for the amount of strain you put on your vocal tract, so you will know when it's too much, when you need to stop what you're doing, and when to take a different approach.

You could alternate high-intensity exercises with lower intensity exercises and songs. I do that all the time when I have a gig in which I have to sing for several hours. As soon as I feel too much strain, I throw in one or two songs that are easy on my voice. After that, I will usually be ready for another high-intensity song. I use low-intensity songs with less required vocal cord closure as a warm-up, and build up toward higher intensity repertoire, which makes sense both from a vocal as well as a performance aspect. Just be smart about what you choose to sing.

And when you do have to sing on high intensity for more extended periods, make sure you get enough rest before you do more. After very long and demanding performances, I always try to give my voice a few days of rest, if at all possible. When this isn't possible, I make sure I do an extra careful warm-up for the next rehearsal or performance that assures I don't get sloppy in regards to technique due to vocal fatigue and general tiredness. Always know where you're at vocally. If you feel hoarseness coming on, be smart about what you do next. Even singing at high intensity can be done in different ways, so make sure you explore all of your options, such as changing vowels or voice color just a little bit to reduce strain, using your support, positioning the larynx, onset, and influencing the ping in your voice. Darkening the voice can cause a lot of strain, so be alert when you feel your general placement change throughout your performance or rehearsal.

How often should you practice?

Master Your Voice

* * *

My rule to determine the best frequency is: as often as you can, as long as your vocal cords permit. The aspect of repetition is hugely important. Repetition is what will help you develop automatisms, and you want to create new automatisms of good singing habits continually, so they work on autopilot. Eventually, more and more aspects of technique will become second nature and you won't have to think about it consciously anymore. There's breathing, posture, support, vocal cord closure, soft palate and pharynx position, and so much more. By now, I don't usually have to think about support, posture, or inhaling deeply anymore. I actually can no longer do it any other way than the way I've trained myself because I've been practicing these habits for such a long time. The more often you do something, the more it sinks into your memory.

So, repeat often, whenever and wherever you can. Also, when you practice regularly, you will figure out much more quickly what doesn't work and what bad habits to drop. When I was studying voice at Southern Methodist University, I would get into a practice room as soon as I had some time between classes, even if it was only 15 minutes. And in that little practice room, I had major breakthroughs. It wasn't usually during my voice lessons with my teacher that the most significant successes happened, but rather during my time of trying to apply what my teacher taught me, which often didn't make any sense until I actually felt it during my own practice time.

Knowing something and doing it are two different things. I would practice my aria, and after 50 times of the high D sounding and feeling tight, the next try suddenly felt different. I had tweaked and tweaked, and suddenly it felt resonant and effortless, the tone was open, had spin, just floated there so beautifully. I kept repeating what I did, and although it didn't work every single time immediately, it became easier all the time and part of my technique. You see, it wasn't easy, because it had taken months of working on this issue, but it only took a moment of feeling the right placement to understand what works. All the work and repetition led to success. The pattern usually goes like this: sing - fail - sing - fail - sing - somewhat get it right - sing - nail it - repeat.

Become an expert and study!

There's so much work you can do without actually singing out loud. Studying and learning more about how the voice works is not only fascinating but will also provide a backbone to the practical application. Knowing what's happening while you sing and what that feels like will help you make faster progress.

As you experiment with your voice, you will know why something you did worked or didn't. Because you have the knowledge, you will know better how to fix a specific problem. So be diligent and study the voice. There are great books, articles, videos, and podcasts that are available, including my own.

WHERE'S YOUR HEART?

Do you find yourself constantly singing, having a tune stuck in your head, writing songs, and just feeling like you're only half a person whenever you don't get to sing and make music? Although my life is pretty much saturated with music and singing, and I absolutely have to take a break to enjoy some time in complete silence every once in a while - which, by the way, is one of the biggest luxuries for me in my life - I couldn't imagine doing anything but talk about music, live in the middle of music, and eat and breathe music every day of my life.

I definitely know what it feels like to work in an environment where you can't act out your musical creativity. Half a lifetime ago, before I became a singer, I worked at an office for a few years. I'm actually a trained and certified travel agent and worked in a nice little travel agency in Frankfurt for a while. I thought that would be an awesome career choice, since I would get to travel and see the world. It didn't really occur to me that the travel agent basically sits in the office all day, eyes glued to a computer screen, selling vacations that he will never take. I did get to take some trips to test hotels and learn about places in the world, but traveling for two weeks a year isn't a lot compared to the many weeks I was stuck at the office.

I found myself writing songs and resenting the music by boss listened to on the radio day in and day out, because it was the same ole same ole... my boss just wasn't an artist and musician like me and listened to music like it's a commodity. I liked him and we got along well. I fact, we're still friends today, and I visit him at the office sometimes. But back then I felt like I was dying on the inside because I couldn't live out my musical creativity. That's when I realized how much it meant to me to be free at any time to work with music, be inspired by music, and create music. I can tell you that nowadays I never get burned out or tired of what I do, although at times I'm physically tired. I have so much energy to put into what I do, simply because it was born out of pure passion. I could not imagine doing anything other than music.

Where is your heart? Can you possibly live without creating music every single day, even when you're tired? Could you accept having a job that pays a lot of money if it meant you had to give up your dream of singing every day? Would you give anything to be able to sing freely whenever you want to? Would you trade a secure job with a nice and steady income for your passion that may not guarantee a steady income?

Even if you don't pursue music full-time now, you know deep in your heart how much space singing takes up in your heart and mind.

Just be honest: when you strip away what people think, what society demands, and any doubts you may have - if you closed your eyes, stripped away all expectations and just saw what's in your heart: what would you want to do with your singing? How much, how often, where, and with whom would you want to sing? What's your ultimate dream? Is it recording your own songs? Or, is it touring with a choir?

I remember sitting in the orchestra pit as a 6-year-old child when my mom played guitar in the orchestra for Rossini's opera „The Barber of Seville", and how much in awe I was. It was a magic world to me, and the ultimate dream I always imagined was me being on stage one day and singing as a soloist with a real symphony orchestra. That dream seemed so huge and crazy back then. I imagined feeling the vibrations of the double basses and timpani and how my voice would just float through space, creating a perfect moment of harmony.

I didn't know that about twenty years later, my dream would become a reality when we had the first rehearsal, or SITZPROBE as we call it in opera theatre, with the orchestra. I sang the lead role of Susanna in Mozart's opera "Le Nozze di Figaro". When the orchestra played the first few pitches, I almost broke out in tears, because I remembered dancing around my room as a child, pretending to sing like an opera singer, and hearing those beautiful sounds of the strings playing while I sang. The moment it became a reality, I knew I could achieve anything in life if I just worked hard and didn't give up on my dreams. I believe my visualizing this scene of singing with an orchestra as a child has a lot to do with it actually happening later.

Even if your dream is just to sing that solo in choir, ask yourself what the cost of never experiencing that moment would be. You may have visualized yourself on stage with everyone's eyes glued on you over and over again, that moment you so strongly long for, when everyone listens to you in silence, and how overwhelming it would feel if your voice was the reason why everyone forgot everything around them for a few moments.

I'm here to tell you that it's all possible! Don't ever think your dream is too big, too crazy, too unrealistic, too lofty! If the Wright brothers had been realistic, there would most likely not be any air travel today, or at least it would have been delayed by many years. Was the landing on the moon realistic? Was Martin Luther King's dream unreasonable?

It's all about your perspective and how much tenacity you have. Is your dream big enough to endure all adversity? It all comes down to what's really in your heart. Just be honest with yourself and admit to yourself and the world how much your dream means to you.

And once you've decided that you absolutely want to do everything you possibly can to make your dream come true - and if you're reading this book, you probably already have - it's just a matter of having a plan and following the steps. I will give you some practical strategies to start the first steps toward your big singing goals. And it doesn't even matter how great your technique is, what voice type you have, how long you've been singing, or how old you are.

The wonderful thing about singing is that every voice is so unique, and finding your uniqueness and capitalizing on it is the true art of being a world-class singer.

I want to help you find that special ingredient in your voice that sets you apart from all the other singers in the world. And yes, you have it in you!

DO YOU NEED A COACH?

While you can learn a lot on your own, essentially no one can do the work for you. However, studying on your own has its limitations. There's a huge benefit of having a personal coach, someone who takes you by the hand and understands your uniqueness and who helps you strengthen your strengths and overcome your weaknesses to where they don't hold you back.

I believe in an approach that combines self-study and coaching, since it will assure you make the most of your knowledge and experience. There's learning time, which you can do with your coach by trying new approaches, learning new aspects, acquiring new knowledge. And there's experimenting time, which you do in your practicing sessions, trying to tweak your sound and find a way to apply all you've learned from your coach.

There are many ways in which you can educate yourself in regards to vocal technique, anatomy, health, and performance skills: there are wonderful books, online courses, and video tutorials on singing. Since there is so much material out there, it's important that you filter through the sheer volume of it all by going with your gut feeling. Honestly, just watching YouTube tutorials on singing can make your head spin in no time. One singer tells you to lower the larynx, the next coach shows how to keep it in a neutral position.

This is the rule: if something makes sense to you and you can feel that it works for you, go for it! If you don't feel the strain and your tone is resonant and free, what you're doing is most likely not wrong. There are wonderful vocal coaches all over the world who create great learning material for singers of all levels and in all genres. However, you want to be sure that the course or tutorial has been created by someone who knows what they're talking about. Of course, you should check out the credentials, but even more importantly, I feel that the way someone sings is indicative of whether they actually practice what they preach and if what they teach is working. It would be hard for me to trust a vocal coach who sounds terrible to my ears and who sounds like he's straining his voice.

Now granted, not every vocal coach has the most beautiful voice, and vice versa, not every great singer can actually teach their skills to others. I believe a good vocal coach has a great level of mastery when it comes to their own vocal technique. How else could he or she demonstrate to the student? Apart from the technique, I can't emphasize enough how important it is that any vocal coach or voice teacher teaches the basic principles of musicality.

Sadly, I hear way too many singers who have beautiful voices, but a high level of musicality is missing. This musicality, however, is exactly what will allow you to move beyond just sounding pretty. There are many singers who have a pretty voice, but actually plunging into the music very deeply and intimately, expressing different levels of dynamics, phrasing in ways that keep the audience in suspense, knowing how to bridge across rests so that tension is maintained, singing clean ad libs that are even and gravitate toward the accented pitches, will all allow you to communicate so much better the essence of what you want to express. There's nothing worse than a singer who sounds the same from the first to the last pitch of the song, in a very monotonous way. This comes across as unemotional and almost robotic. Expressiveness is often more important than absolute perfection.

Nowadays, there are many ways to find a great vocal coach. You can contact your local music school, or ask at a college in your city if there are voice classes available. Sometimes the voice teachers who teach at community colleges also give private lessons. Or, if you're looking for a top-notch teacher, faculty or adjunct faculty may be willing to take on external students if they are intrigued by their talent. Asking doesn't cost anything.

You can also do a Google search to find local voice teachers. Take a look at the newspaper, there may be an advertisement of a local music school or voice teacher who is accepting new students. If you live in a more remote area where you can't find an excellent voice teacher, there's always the internet. Many very renowned teachers offer lessons via Skype, which means you can take lessons in the comfort of your home, skipping the travel time to a studio. You may also find a teacher you totally fall in love with, for instance on Youtube or Udemy, and there's a good chance they also offer online one-on-one lessons. Check out their websites for more info.

Once you've found someone to take lessons from, give yourself and your new teacher time to get to know each other before you decide if it's a good fit. It may take a few weeks to develop trust and allow yourself to completely open up. After all, the voice is a very personal matter, and anytime anyone asks you to make sounds that sound a little crazy at times and being completely vulnerable, it takes a lot of confidence to do that in front of a complete stranger. But you should begin to feel comfortable in the presence of your voice teacher after a short period.

If you feel like you're always holding back, you may have to look for someone who makes it easier for you to experiment and be bold. Ask yourself though if it's your personality or your teacher making you feel uncomfortable. I've had students who felt comfortable in my presence, but were generally very shy, so that took some time to work through.

Once you've found a teacher you click with, you should keep track of your progress. I recommend you record every lesson. That way, you can listen to the lesson between sessions, sing along with the exercises - since they're sometimes easily forgotten, and listen to yourself objectively. The way you perceive your voice while you sing is not what others hear.

Sometimes your teacher may have told you to make a change, and you couldn't hear the difference while you were actually doing it. You will always perceive your voice differently than someone listening from the outside. Your ears just happen to be inside your head, which means the sound you hear while you sing isn't precisely what others perceive. You listen to yourself partially from the inside. Keep your recordings at hand so that you can check after a few months if there's an improvement. You should hear some noticeable improvements after a few months.

It's really cool to come across old recordings and realize that there has been a drastic change for the better. If after about a year you have the feeling you're not making any progress, or even worse, feel like you are getting more confused, and your voice is continuously strained, you may have to ditch your teacher and look for someone else. While one teacher may be a perfect fit for one singer and truly help them improve, they may not be a good fit for another singer.

When I studied voice at Southern Methodist University, I was very blessed to have a teacher who happened to be perfect for me. Prof. Barbara Hill Moore brought out the best in me and understood my voice as well as my personality. However, she may not have been the best fit for everyone.

If you don't click with a teacher, this does not mean the teacher isn't a great teacher per se, it just indicates that he or she may not hear in your voice what will help you achieve more ease and the most beautiful sound.

You should beware of a teacher who makes every single one of their students sound the same, uses the same approach, and just tends to teach in a way that results in clones of their own voice. Everyone's voice is unique and different, and a good voice teacher should respect and admire that. It's his/her job to help you bring out that uniqueness.

I have learned a lot over the years as a vocal coach, and the most important thing was that what works for one student, doesn't necessarily work for another student. I always have to come up with new exercises on the fly, experimenting with what works for that particular singer. That's what I love so much about teaching voice. It's a continuous challenge, and I love hearing new voice colors emerge as we explore new sounds.

A good voice teacher should encourage you to try new approaches, while at the same time guiding you toward a solid foundation for a healthy technique.

I have seen voice teachers who don't even know that they only sing in head voice. How then can they teach their students the different registers and transitions? I have also had students who have been classified as an alto by their voice teachers, but who apparently have a bright and high voice. After they had been taught to sing in a dark voice color and everything in low keys, the students almost gave up, because it did not feel right and was even very uncomfortable. Some were taught to always sing higher although they clearly struggled even after much practice. After working with me for a while, singing in their natural voice, they discovered a never before felt ease and actually enjoyed singing more than ever, because they knew this was their voice and it's supposed to sound that way. It didn't constantly feel strained but free instead.

If you have the feeling that your voice teacher is pushing you in a direction you think is totally wrong and not YOU, you should talk to him or her about it. Have them explain their approach and why they think this approach works and where it is supposed to lead you. I always try to help my students understand why we do specific exercises so that all we do makes sense overall. It will also help them continue learning on their own when they don't take lessons anymore, and that's what I want them to be able to.

Understanding the grand plan, if you will, is beneficial both for the student and teacher. It's like learning to read: in the beginning, you need a lot of guidance and correction, but once you understand the basics and how the system works, you can read almost anything, even words you haven't seen before.

The more experience you gain, the more fluent you become, and the more complex texts you can read and comprehend. Singing is very similar once you have understood certain concepts and rules. Knowing why and how the voice works will enable you to troubleshoot any future problems. If your teacher helps you with this process, it's perfect.

In hindsight, I understand so much more about why my teacher wanted me to do certain things, while at the time they often didn't make sense to me and even caused frustration. I now know that sometimes, to change old habits that hold you back, you need to go to the other extreme. For example, if you have a very soft and small voice and always sing in a very narrow and breathy tone, it may help to sing in a darker tone with lots of jaw movement to give you a sense of what's possible. I often ask my students to do something extreme on the scale of darkness or brightness so they feel how far is all the way and then can utilize the middle much better.

Remember that singing isn't just physical, it's also psychological.

Having a coach will most likely allow you to make much faster progress than studying on your own. You have someone to hold you accountable, who also has lots of experience and knows how to guide you so you can avoid detours.

HUSTLE AND REST

It's true that in order to become excellent in what you do, you have to put in many, many hours of practicing. It is said that it takes ten thousand hours of doing something until you become an expert. Now, you may think, if I just put in ten hours every day, I will be an expert in a little more than three years. While the math may be correct, it's not that easy. Your brain isn't designed to always work equally efficient every day. Being intentional and respecting your natural tendencies for learning make a big difference.

I'm sure you've experienced this: you had all the best intentions to study a little bit every day before an exam, but you kept procrastinating and suddenly realized that you only had one day left to cram in all of the material. You pulled an all-nighter, with a pitcher of coffee to help you through, and barely made it to the exam, because you were exhausted and got zero sleep. You didn't do so bad on the test, but all the material you studied overnight seemed to be gone yet again overnight.

Our brains are made so that we need periods of rest to transform anything we've learned or experienced into long term memories.

You see, the principle of rest is also an essential part of the equation in becoming a master of your voice. Since your body is your instrument and singing is not just about learning cognitively, you need that time between practice sessions to rest so that first of all, your voice can rest and recover (unfortunately, or actually, fortunately, you don't have vocal cords of steel), and second of all learning takes place when the brain has time to process information so it can settle into long-term memory.

Any athlete can tell you that peak performance is only possible with the right amount of rest time between training periods and competition days.

In singing, rest is just as important as taking action. I sometimes have days and weeks when I have to do a lot of singing. I teach my students, which means I demonstrate every exercise at least once, plus many parts of the songs we work on. Then there are rehearsals for my gigs, the warm-ups I do for my rehearsals and concerts, plus the gigs themselves. Sometimes I have up to four performances in a single week, or even two on the same day, some of which require several hours of singing. I have a lot of stamina because I have trained my voice for many years, but I definitely can't go on and on like the Duracell bunny. After periods with a lot of singing, it does wonders to do absolutely no singing for a while and, if possible, even take a couple of weeks off if I can. My voice feels so refreshed and free then, because it's had time to rest and recuperate.

Don't worry: you don't forget how to sing even if you rest for a few days or weeks. Besides, you use your voice every day. Your speaking voice is the same voice you use for singing, without putting quite such high demands on it as in singing. Another aspect is getting physical rest since singing is literally a workout for your whole body. And mind. Getting enough sleep after some short nights will help you recharge and sharpen your senses.

Taking a break is also important when memorizing your repertoire. Your memory is a lot more efficient when you alternate between periods of focus and periods of rest. Also, when you study a song, it's very beneficial to put it down for a few weeks or months and come back to it later. In my studio, I usually work on a song with a student for several weeks and get into a lot of technical detail as well as matters of interpretation and performance. We then let it rest for a while, and after a few weeks sing through it again. Almost every single time, something wonderful happens: there's a lot more ease and flow because my student doesn't over think everything as much. Most of the things we talked about just happen naturally and everything makes a lot more sense.

It's like the saying that you sometimes can't see the forest because of all the trees. Songs do take some time to settle into your voice and memory. Plus, once you know a song by heart, you don't focus as much on remembering the melody, lyrics, and counts. You begin singing more intuitively, which is the key to connecting to the music to interpret it in your own unique way.

There's another type of rest that is also essential: allow moments of silence in your performance. Don't be afraid to take your time, don't ever rush when it's not necessary. A rest or moment of silence can create a wonderful instance of suspense for your audience that draws them to you because they wonder what comes next. I see singers who get hectic way too often. For example, once the song has ended, don't break the tension by falling out of character or just belittling what just happened in the music. Don't be embarrassed to take all the time in the world when appropriate, and generously accept your audience's recognition. Allow yourself to bathe in the applause since it comes across as rude and ungrateful when you rush off the stage or just move on without acknowledging and being grateful.

Take your time to breathe whenever you can. Use the rests in the music to let your breath flow naturally to become part of the sound. And whenever there is a fermata, dare to take your time holding that pitch - or rest. Silence is also sound. Imagine music only consisting of sounds and no rests. For our brains to understand where one section ends and another begins, we sometimes need moments of silence. There's an effect of positive surprise when a singer holds that last high note for much longer than expected. Take a coffee break on that pitch if you can do it technically and if it's appropriate. I always love people's faces when I hold that high pitch in a cadenza of an opera aria for what seems like an eternity. They always break out in applause without fail.

You have to learn the concept that in music silence is sound. And love the moments of silence as well as rest.

STRATEGIES AND ROUTINES

In order to achieve your goals to become the best singer you can be, you need a battle plan you can execute, some kind of road map if you will that will lead you to your end destination. I see way too many singing students who have taken lessons for years, but who don't know where they stand and where they're going. Some can't even name the problems they are dealing with. It's just one huge gray area of "my voice sounds bad," and the goal is just a general "I want to become a better singer."

I always teach my students not just to judge their voices and divide everything into the two categories of "this sounds good" or "this sounds terrible." I instead want them to become a critic who can describe why something sounds good or bad. When you define the quality of sound, for instance as narrow, pressed, raspy, dark, you may have already found the solution. You don't get discouraged, because as soon as you identify the sound quality of your voice, you also can describe what it is that is unpleasing to your ears, and consequently prescribe a strategy on how to make the necessary changes to improve the sound and feeling.

For instance, let's assume you sing a long, high pitch in head voice, and you just hate the sound of it. It also doesn't feel right because it feels very strained. Instead of just getting frustrated because it doesn't sound or feel like you want it to, try to find the root of the problem. You may find that the tone quality is very narrow, that there isn't any silvery sound, no spin, no ping, no overtones, and just no brilliance in the tone. The reason for a narrow pressed sound is often caused by a lack of resonating space or too much tension. You may need to lift your soft palate more, relax your jaw and make sure you have good breath support. Maybe you're pushing too much air through your vocal folds which results in breathiness, which in turn makes you press even more. When you make changes according to your prescribed solution, you will be able to project more, and your tone will open up and sound a lot more open and resonant without feeling strained.

I like writing down a problem, then formulating a battle plan of exercises to help me improve, including setting a deadline by which I want to have mastered the issue. It's definitely helpful to have a system in place that works for you. It may be listening to recordings of yourself, maybe even videos, or listening to singers who have the desired sound qualities you are working on.

To be qualified to become your own critic, you should begin following some routines so you can develop essential automatisms.

If you want to perform at your best, here are some things to consider:

Take care of your instrument
Since your body is your instrument, it's imperative that you treat your body with the utmost care and respect. When your body feels weak, so will your voice. So the first necessary step to keep your voice healthy and working well is to keep your body healthy, strong and fresh.

In the past, a lot of people thought that only singers with a large body could sing opera since big bodies must produce big sounds. However, the truth actually is that the most important thing is a healthy and fit body. Whether you're very thin or have a few pounds extra isn't what decides over the quality of your voice. It's the level of fitness that will allow you strength and stamina.

Singing requires your body to support a very controlled breath and have a general tension at all times. For that, you definitely need some muscles, especially around your mid-section, where all of the muscles that control your inhalation and exhalation are located.

Exercising regularly not only improves your quality of life because you just feel better, but it also helps you to have a strong body to support those high notes, those long passages that require a lot of control, and those very soft passages that need to be hugely supported by your abdominal and back muscles. If you've ever sung through a whole show, you know how physically taxing this can be - if you've really given it your all without holding back.

There are a few more things you should consider to keep your voice working at its best:

Drink enough water

First of all, keeping your body sufficiently hydrated will assure that it can perform all of its primary functions to keep you alive and stay healthy. Logically, when your body is in a state of alert because of dehydration, it will naturally direct all focus to essential functions, but not to anything that's not necessary to sustain your life. Your level of hydration also affects the performance of your vocal cords. When your body is dehydrated, your vocal cords also get dry and don't work at peak efficiency. It's best to drink water throughout the day, making sure you maintain a good level of hydration at all times. If you've forgotten to drink, it isn't very effective to just drink five glasses of water and gulp them down quickly to „catch up", since your body can't absorb it and will just flush out any liquids that it doesn't use. A good indicator if you are drinking enough water is the color of your urine. One of my teachers who taught vocal pedagogy class always said "pee pale"! Also, when you feel thirsty, it's already a sign that you're dehydrated.

Since after a good night's sleep, you haven't hydrated for at least eight hours, it's a good idea to start the day with a glass of water. Again, drinking small quantities throughout the day consistently is much better than drinking huge amounts at once, which will only have you running to the bathroom over and over again.

Eat a healthy and balanced diet

What I'm telling you here is just common sense. If you eat junk, you will feel like junk! Make sure you stay away from processed foods as much as possible and eat fresh fruit, vegetables, and meats. As a busy performer, I've learned about the value of quality foods to help my body perform at its best and keep energy levels up. I feel so much better when I eat good foods with lots of valuable nutrients and without too many empty calories that just make you feel sluggish and are hard on your digestive system. When I have hectic days or weeks and know that I will be traveling, I make sure I don't get into situations in which I eat junk food out of despair.

I know the feeling: after a gig, it's usually late, and it's been hours since the last meal or snack, and your fuel tanks are running on empty. You still have a couple of hours before you get home and you're wound up from all the excitement of the evening. Don't let yourself go hungry since that will most likely cause you to make bad food choices when you get

„hangry". I avoid 2 AM stops at McDonald's drive-thru by packing some good stuff I can dig into. I always take cut up some vegetables like carrots, celery, bell peppers, tomatoes, avocados, radishes, and cucumbers and have a small jar of homemade yogurt dip made from plain greek yogurt, olive oil, apple cider vinegar, salt, pepper, and some herbs waiting for me. Not only is this a delicious and practical snack you can eat as finger food, but it's great for your body. Plain nuts are also wonderful, as well as homemade energy balls made of oats, dates, chia seeds, chopped cashews, and a little honey or maple syrup.

I also take lots of fruit that's in season, and that's easy to eat on the go, like apples, pears, bananas, plums, berries, peaches, nectarines, and grapes. These may be higher in sugar, but it's infinitely better to pig out on fruit than wedding cake with heaps of frosting. Besides the sugar in fruit, you also get lots of great nutrients, vitamins, and fiber. You can eat these in a car, on the train, or on an airplane. Especially on long plane flights, I find that I prefer to eat a lot more than the meals that get served. I never eat the rolls made of white flour and stay away from yogurts with lots of added sugar. So it's a great idea to take a stash of fruits and veggies to satisfy the munchies when you feel them coming on. Especially on long flights, I make sure I drink lots of water, since the dry air in the plane dries out my body so much quicker than in an environment with normal humidity levels.

I also take along a little Ziploc bag with cut up fresh ginger along with a thermos cup. All I need to do then is go to the galley and ask for hot water. Fresh ginger tea is excellent to calm an upset stomach or any nausea, and it also strengthens your immune system.

Eat whatever you want as long as it's fresh, doesn't come out of a factory and has good nutrient density.

If you know that you are sensitive to some foods, avoid them. Everybody is different, and so you will have to take on the responsibility to give your body the best nutrition possible. You may want to experiment with a few foods if you notice that you have a lot of phlegm after eating certain foods. Some people are sensitive towards dairy products or spicy food. Try to cut that food out of your diet and see if there's a change. I'm very blessed not to have any reactions to any foods whatsoever, but I know not everybody is as lucky as I am.

Exercise regularly

You know that you just feel different when you do some physical activity on a regular basis instead of being a couch potato most of the time. Your mental sharpness also increases when you exercise. Singing is very demanding on your body and mind, so you want to make sure you're in the best condition to deliver on a high level.

I've heard the argument many times that there's just no time to exercise. But let me tell you that my experience is that I'm so much more productive and can focus so much better when I have exercised. You can't afford to not do it. Besides, getting sick takes up a lot more time and money.

I would recommend getting into a daily routine of exercising. It doesn't have to be long or very taxing. Just start with small things like going for a brisk walk uphill, or swimming in the summer, doing some yoga, stretching, or body weight workouts. These are free ways to strengthen your body, and you don't need a gym nor a lot of time. You can slowly increase your pace and duration and build up your endurance. And endurance is something you will need if you want to perform on stage. I see way too many singers who start out a performance strong and push themselves to the limit during the first fifteen minutes, only to start singing with a compromised technique after a short while because they have no more strength left to continue at that high level.

Your overall fitness will help you with your breathing, support, and body awareness. Singing is hard physical work. Exercising will also clear up your mind and help your brain to work more efficiently. You will be able to focus much better and to memorize lyrics more easily.

Alternating days on which you do aerobic exercises, such as running, swimming, and biking, with days on which you do anaerobic exercises, such as weight training is perfect for building both strength and endurance, and ultimately, feel better and live a healthier life.

Pay attention to your speaking voice

You should get into the habit of being more aware of the way you use your voice throughout the day. Since your singing and speaking voice essentially use the same parts, one influences the other. When you go to a party or a concert, be careful not to strain your voice too much by yelling loudly for extended periods. You're going to hate it if you can't sing for a few days simply because you overdid it for a few hours. As a singer, you want to be more conscious about the way you use your resources.

You also should be aware of your speaking pitch. If you feel your voice getting hoarse or tired quickly when you speak at a normal volume level, you should ask yourself if you speak in an area of your voice that's too high or too low for your natural voice. Your speaking technique can affect your singing voice a lot. If you suspect you have problems with your speaking voice in general and that something isn't quite right - for instance, if you always have a breathy tone or break easily - you may want to see a speech therapist or have your vocal cords checked by an ear, nose and throat doctor. I've had students who had poor vocal cord closure already in their speaking voice. Some were diagnosed with an asymmetry of their vocal cords or general weakness in the muscles that are needed for proper cord closure and were prescribed treatment by a speech therapist. Always make sure your voice is generally healthy, as some problems may stem from a condition that can't be fixed merely by improving your singing technique.

Get enough quality sleep

This is something that is sometimes hard to follow through on, primarily as a performing artist who often has gigs late in the day or even until long after midnight. It's normal to have concerts and gigs that sometimes run very late, not including the socializing afterward plus taking care of equipment and drive home for a few hours. That's just the nature of a singer's job. You perform at other people's leisure time.

However, you don't have that same demanding schedule every single day of the week, and on those days that don't allow you to get a good night's sleep, you need to plan in a day or two afterward to help your body recharge, if possible. When you're tired, your technique automatically deteriorates, simply because you can't focus as well and don't have the physical strength. Your support isn't continuous anymore, and your vocal cords tend to not close as tightly, only because your tired body can't create the muscle tension to keep it up.

It's not so much what you do on any one given day as the everyday lifestyle that adds up. You can survive on several days with little to no sleep, but this isn't anything I would recommend on a regular basis. Every time you don't give your body what it needs, it's like taking a little bit away from your health savings. You can withdraw some here and there and put it back a day later. But making poor food choices, drinking alcohol, smoking, stressing, or sleep deprivation eat away on your overall strength and weaken your immune system.

Find the perfect warm-up routine for your voice

Every voice is different, and while some basic principles apply to everyone, you may find that some exercises work better for you than others. Your voice is unique, so you need to find out exactly what works best. You may find out that on different days different exercises feel more or less effective, depending on the condition of your voice and how much you have been using your voice on that day or the day before. I have days when I am warmed up very quickly, and on other days, I feel that my vocal cords are a little tense, so I take more time on lower to mid-range exercises to make sure I help my vocal cords operate at a level of ideal efficiency before demanding too much like belting out loud and high in heavy mechanism.

You also may want to come up with new exercises to challenge your voice in new and different ways. It's always fun to try new things and to create exercises on the spot to help your voice master challenges it may have that moment. It does get tiresome to do the same exercises over and over again, although I find that there are some top 5 exercises I always like to use because they always work well for me. Taylor the exercises according to your range and the challenges you're currently working on.

Sing smart

We already talked about the fact that your voice isn't the same every single day. You know by now that some days are better than others. That's why you need to learn to assess how much is too much or how much is enough as far as intensity and strain are concerned. You need to turn on your sensors to warn you when there's too much strain, or when you're not putting forth enough effort.

Make sure you alternate between songs that are very taxing and songs that actually help your vocal cords and body relax a little. Some songs are naturally less straining than others. Even in your practice or coaching sessions, express to your coach or co musicians when you feel too much strain that is uncomfortable. Ask someone to turn your mic up, or if the male singer of the band can take a turn so you can rest for a couple of songs.

However, there is a fine line between challenging yourself - and yes, singing IS hard work - and overdoing it to where you actually hurt your vocal cords. That's why you must learn to feel the difference. You don't need to become paranoid, but it's so important to know what it feels like when you're not just pushing your vocal cords to grow, but when you're potentially doing damage. You could sing any given song in so many different ways, depending on the shape of your voice that day.

Whenever I have had a long singing week and know my voice is already tired, but I have yet another 4-hour gig to pull through, I don't sing with maximum intensity the whole time. I take everything back just a tiny notch, get into head voice a little bit sooner, and just don't push the volume as much. When I have a gig where I provide background music, it's absolutely legitimate and even necessary to sing with a softer voice, in contrast to a performance with a big orchestra, where I'm the main attraction singing two feature songs as a highlight, which must be sung perfectly and all out. Just be smart about the way you sing at all times. You do want to be able to still sing with a clear voice 10, 20, and 30 years from now. You can't get a new voice, so take care of the one you have at any cost.

Sometimes it's already helpful to change the singing approach of a few pitches if a song permits it to reduce the workload on your vocal cords just a little. I always try to find even the tiniest opportunities to make it a little easier here and there, especially in sets where there are ten or more very difficult and high songs in sequence. If you engage your voice a little bit like a rubber band, stretching and releasing, without keeping everything too static with the same pressure, color, and dynamic level, you won't get tired as quickly. Your body doesn't want to be static.

Remember you only have one voice, one pair of vocals cords. You can't buy new ones, and you can't just repair them easily once they've been damaged. Having focal fold surgery is risky, and the healing process takes time. You can't just put on a new set of strings for the next gig. You must always protect your voice to ensure you will have it for the rest of your life, keeping its full range alive.

Don't sing extremely straining songs for an extended period - take a break if you feel you are getting raspy. Just be smart and pay attention to how your voice feels and decide for yourself what you can or cannot handle vocally.

If you get sick

If you happen to get sick, which unfortunately happens to all of us, take your time to get well. Don't take any strong prescription medications if you just have a common cold. Try to use natural remedies that help your body help itself. The best cure for a cold is simple: rest and time. Your body will heal itself if you just let it and don't interfere too much. There are excellent natural remedies that help alleviate symptoms.

If you have a raspy throat because of a cold, drink ginger tea made with fresh ginger root, or sage tea with honey. Cough drops with menthol tend to dry out your throat, so it's better not to use them. While the best thing you can do for your voice when you're sick is just to give it rest, once you feel you're getting better you should get back into a vocalization routine slowly and carefully.

Once you feel your voice is getting better, start vocalizing on very soft low to mid-range pitches that are hummed. Make sure there's no breathiness since this puts strain on your vocal cords and will irritate them and potentially cause a setback. Do those first singing vocalizations after a cold for a few days, slowly increasing intensity and pitch, before you actually start singing full out again. That way you make sure your vocal cords are ready to be put to work again. Also, keep in mind that speaking is often a lot more taxing on your vocal cords than singing. Speak as little as possible, and don't whisper, since this also causes strain.

As a professional performer, I sometimes can't take the time to rest when I'm sick and have to perform anyway. Keep in mind we're talking about a common cold here, not the flu. Whenever I have to sing with a cold, I try to be smart. I don't speak but just try to limit my vocalizations to what is absolutely necessary (a very focused and concise warm-up and the performance itself).

I drink lots of warm tea with honey. The best throat lozenges I have found for singers that really help the voice are GeloRevoice. They are really awesome, and I use them whenever I feel raspiness coming on and know I have to perform. If I take them throughout my performance day, they really help prevent hoarseness and the urge to cough, and at least my voice doesn't get worse by singing. They are manufactured in Germany, but you can also buy them on Amazon in the U.S. and other countries.

Sage cough drops are also very effective, as well as an herbal gargle made of thyme, sage, eucalyptus, cinnamon, clove, and anise essential oils. It has anti-inflammatory properties and maintains the physiological balance of mouth bacteria.

I put the gargle mixture into an empty water bottle and take it with me on the way to my gig. I just keep gargling every 20-30 minutes, and this has been very helpful to me on occasions when my voice was almost gone due to a cold. There's one ready-made gargle with the above-mentioned ingredients named Salviathymol, but it's not always available outside of Europe. You can mix your own if you combine those essential oils though.

I also try to choose my repertoire intelligently. If possible, I try to start with the lower, less intense, softer pieces. By the time I work myself up to the more difficult pieces, my voice has warmed up without too much of a preceding warmup and often times actually gotten better by the time the first low-intensity song is over. I have indeed already experienced my voice being all raspy at the beginning of a gig, and afterward, it was so much better. Singing with proper technique and intelligently actually helped my voice get better. When you slowly massage your vocal cords by singing the first song of the set as a warm-up with particular attention to detail, you may not even need a warm-up before that. It's a good idea to have two or three songs in mind which you can use as such a warm-up for those times when you need it.

Again, I want to emphasize that we're talking about singing with a common cold. There are definitely more severe conditions which do not permit you to use your voice at all. If you have laryngitis and continue to vocalize (singing or speaking), you may do serious damage to your vocal cords. If you're not sure about the nature of your raspiness or hoarseness, you should see an ENT. Sometimes there's no way around vocal rest.

Set goals and make a plan

I know it can feel overwhelming to realize all the things you need to work on: there's breathing correctly, improving your posture, getting that tension out of your neck, relaxing your jaw, opening your throat, coloring the vowels just right, getting the ping into your voice, increasing your range on the top and bottom, lifting your soft palate, smoothing out transitions, increasing your range in chest voice, practicing whistle register, and so much more. It's hard to know where to start and lose track of your progress. It also makes you a little anxious while you actually sing, because you're trying to keep so many things in mind. You focus on an open throat, and there goes your support, which you had just managed so nicely. You focus on the vowel to get better resonance, and you forget to breathe deeply. It's just so frustrating. Let me tell you: you're totally normal! You just need to make a plan to follow, and you will be well on your way of actually getting more productive in your practice time to get closer to your goals. Work on one thing at a time and be ok with taking small steps.

Focus on one issue that comes up within a song and work on it strategically. For instance, if you have a song that gives you trouble regarding your breath control and you find yourself out of breath all the time, gasping for air, you should circle in on that problem and start at the basics.

First, you should assess your posture: do you have a good posture that allows you to breathe freely and entirely without constrictions? Do you inhale deeply enough, so your lungs are fully inflated? Is there good rib expansion? Do you have good vocal cord closure when you sing, or is there excessive breathiness, which causes your air to be lost all too quickly? Do you breathe too late and therefore too hastily before your entrances and therefore don't take a deep enough breath? Do you even know where to take a breath? Do you forget to breathe and then run out of air? Should you breathe more or less often in the song?

Not breathing at the right frequency can create a vicious cycle, since taking shallow breaths means not inhaling enough air, running out of air quickly, and usually singing with insufficient support, which promotes inadequate vocal cord closure and more breathiness, which means you will run out of air even more rapidly in the next few measures. You get fatigued very quickly and struggle more and more. You should sing from the top of your breath rather than the bottom. You know how bad it feels when you don't ever get the chance to breathe deeply and continuously find yourself out of breath after just a few pitches, and even when you breathe, you still don't take in enough air because you're gasping and rushing.

Taking it back to the basics and reminding yourself of a good breathing technique and perfect posture over and over again will help you get to the root of the problem so you can work on it more intentionally. If the problem stems from inhaling too shallowly, you may just want to do some exercises that help you take your time and breathe more deeply. Next, you may want to begin vocalizing and breathing very deeply and efficiently in between phrases.

After you feel comfortable doing this, you may want to go back to your song and write down some breathing marks to plan out exactly when you will take a breath. This will help you anticipate how long the air you inhale should last and you can sing the pitches accordingly. I would isolate phrases that present the most difficulties and practice those specifically, even at a lowered tempo to help you develop some automatisms. Then you could increase the tempo, and finally, sing through the whole song.

Break down the phrase and create exercises with those pitches, vowels, and transitions. This approach is so much more effective than singing through a song over and over again, exhausting your voice and creating a lot of frustration, because there seem to be an infinite amount of problems. However, the truth is that it could just be two problems that keep repeating. So, each time you sing the chorus, that issue comes up. It may only be a small thing to fix, but if you don't address it, it will continue to cause frustration.

Always try to diagnose the root of the problem and go from there until you've worked out the kinks. Once you improve in one area, you can move on to address other issues. Your brain just can't process too many things at once. Multitasking is a myth, believe me. Once you do something over and over again, it becomes an automatism, and you don't have to think about it consciously. You will find that this will happen more and more as you work on specific problems and target them intentionally.

Although I always correct my students on many levels, I remind them that our lesson only serves to identify the problems and prescribe a way to fix them. The actual work starts when they go home and practice on their own. By mentioning the same things over and over again, they begin remembering more and more, until eventually things become second nature and develop into habits. That's the point when they don't have to think about what to do anymore consciously. Only to then focus on another issue that needs work.

I have created a Goal Tracking Sheet for Singers that you can download for free on my website at www.masteryourvoice.tv. It helps you focus on a specific problem and set a date by which you want to be able to have mastered the issue you're working on. You will pick a song to work on and exercises to help you improve. It's great to have a visual plan since it motivates you and creates some sort of road map to follow. You will know every day what to practice, what exercises to do, and how much time you should invest to reach your goal.

HOW TO FIND YOUR UNIQUENESS

When you think of any brand that is well known, it's very recognizable, has a clear message, and you could just tell me instantly what makes the product unique. When you think of Coca Cola, you instantly think of a red and white font and can almost taste the sparkling sweetness in your mouth. You could also tell me that the message the brand communicates is something along the lines of fun, freedom, friends, and good times. Of course, we've all seen the commercials around Christmas time in which the whole world seems to unite in peace to celebrate the existence of Coke.

As a singer, it is equally important to define yourself as a brand. You have to know what it is that sets you apart from any other singer, and what your audience has come to expect from you. Is it your vulnerability and tenderness that draws others in, or is it your power and unusual conviction in your songs? You need to know the message you want to communicate and the emotions you want your audience to associate you with. Do they want to listen to you because they just want to feel good and get in a good mood, or do they want to become part of deep emotions to empathize with you and identify with some of the pain you sing about? Or both?

When you think of any very successful singer, they have not only mastered the art of singing, but they also have a clear brand they stand for.

Michael Jackson was the master of pop, dance, and choreography in combination with a breathtaking live stage show. He was a perfectionist when it comes to the flow of the show, the music arrangements, the individual musicians, and the distinct sound of the guitar because he had a clear vision of the experience he wanted to deliver to his audience. Because he was so clear about it, his audience always knew they could expect a show that was the most amazing experience they could imagine, packed with breathtaking surprises.

On the other hand, when you think of Eva Cassidy, you probably think of intimacy, beauty, vulnerability, tenderness, and emotions. Acoustic music that's unedited, personal, and authentic. All she needed was her voice and her guitar, and she could draw the audience in by making them part of her world for a while. You want to listen to her because she communicates the essence of being simply human. But she does this in a very pure and raw way, so there's no expectation of any spectacular effects or even flow to the show other than listening to someone who has stories to tell. Real life stories.

Do you see how much one singer can differ from another, but still be absolutely amazing? However, finding exactly what it is that your audience really wants and expects from you, isn't an easy undertaking. It will probably take you years to keep refining your own definition of who you are as an artist, but it is an essential part of your success. It's all about recognizing your strengths and building on them.

You may have noticed people telling you what they loved the most whenever you performed. Since the way you perceive yourself is often not at all the way others view you, it is beneficial and an absolute must to ask others about their opinions and thoughts about what they love most about your voice, personality, and stage performance. Is it the sheer beauty of your voice, or is it the edginess? Is it your ability to connect to the audience on a very emotional level, or is it your dance moves that groove along with the beat while you sing with power and authority? Or do you have the superpower to spread fun and make everyone dance and sing along and rock the party?

Keep asking your audience what they love the most, and what they thought you could leave out or improve on. It's always good to have an honest friend tell you the truth. You will get a great sense about what defines you as a singer. However, don't give the opinion of one person too much importance. It's the common thread that you will find after getting consistent feedback from friends, family, those who have seen you perform for the first time, and musician colleagues.

Always be aware of the fact that your personality has everything to do with your voice, and your voice expresses your personality. If you are a very sweet and shy person, this will be expressed in the way you perform, your posture, and the sound of your voice. If, on the other hand, you are bold and unwavering, you will undoubtedly transport that in your voice and the way you perform.

I do this exercise in my Online Masterclass for Singers to help every singer find their unique and recognizable brand. First, they have to tell everyone in class what they think defines themselves as an artist. That's usually a tough task for most because it's hard to say something really great about yourself. But being convinced about what makes you special and unique is basically what you have to do when it comes to selling yourself as a brand. We're all taught to be modest, but there's nothing immodest about recognizing one's strengths.

Then I ask everyone else in the group to tell that singer what they like best about that other singer and what they would want more or less of as an audience. Since everyone is also a singer, they can put it into words much better than someone who doesn't know how to describe voice quality or presentation skills as a performer. It's always amazing how everything falls into place after everyone has essentially told that singer what they love most about them. That singer usually begins choosing repertoire that falls right in line with that definition, and they gain so much clarity on what to work on and what direction to go since there are literally a million things you could do as a singer. It's good to know what to focus on and what will be your bread and butter. The format of a masterclass is so helpful because there's so much to be learned by watching others and even critiquing others and prescribing solutions. It really helps your creativity and skill to listen and hear flaws or great qualities in others, which enables you to realize that you do some of those things yourself.

I have learned a great deal in masterclasses, watching how someone else is being coached by the master. In my masterclass, the members have access to all of the recordings of our sessions on video, so they can go back, watch themselves and revisit some of the issues we addressed. Everyone can benefit from the suggestions given to any other singer and utilize those same critiques to improve their own technique.

It's very encouraging to know that others have exactly the same problems you have and that these issues are not insurmountable, but with some tenacity and work, can be overcome. Video is absolutely great for future reference, which is why I recommend you record yourself on video from time to time. You can always go back and have an objective comparison to the way you sang then and what has changed for the better. It's very motivating to watch old videos of yourself and find you don't struggle with those same problems anymore.

The best person to learn from is someone who already does what you want to become good at, who has already walked the path to success. An experienced coach and performer knows what's relevant when it comes to performance skills, and can help you find that special sauce. So you always want to learn from people you admire and who have the qualities you hope to make your own. Always surround yourself with people who are better than you, which will push you a lot harder than being the best in a group. To achieve greatness, you must look at people who are already great.

Listening to excellent singers with great technique will give you an ear for a desirable sound, and you will subconsciously imitate some of their good qualities, and at the same time make them your own without copying. Every artist out there has been influenced by other artists, and that's a very good thing. You want to take the best from all the great singers and create something new from it that is uniquely you.

The advantage of having a teacher and mentor who has already gone through the whole process to get where you also want to go is that he can make you aware of all the obstacles they've encountered and mistakes they've made. You will make much faster progress than when you study on your own. I wish that when I began my journey as a singer, someone would have told me how to do so many things, like what equipment to use, how to make a good recording, and how I should make myself known to agencies and venues. You just don't know these things when you've never done them.

While everything you can learn is mainly about doing it yourself and learning through trial and error, you can potentially speed up the learning process by getting someone to help you around some obstacles that otherwise just take a lot of time to figure out.

Someone who has the experience in the business can help you find your uniqueness and what it is that you need to sell. After all, you're only really successful when you have an audience who wants what you have to give. The process of finding out what it is that makes you unique, is a continuous work in progress, as you always keep morphing into the best artist you can be at any given time. Your best five years ago will not be the same as your best today, as you keep on learning and developing your skills, likes and dislikes. There are songs I used to sing all the time, but my taste shifted a little and some of those old pieces I can't stand anymore. I like lots of depth nowadays, and there's nothing technical that can keep me from singing a difficult piece of music.

As you continue to be influenced by your experiences and other musicians, and especially your own life's story, you will continuously become a more refined and defined artist.

When I listen to recordings or watch videos of myself singing 10 years ago, I sometimes have to cringe. I almost can't believe some of the technical flaws I displayed, which by now have mostly disappeared. Technique has become routine. Of course, there are other flaws, but it's wonderful to see that I have reached a completely different level of mastery, even in the way I move and gesture. The way I carry myself on stage has changed so much - I have so much more confidence, which doesn't only have an effect on my professional success, but also on my personal life. I have learned never to be embarrassed to be myself.

That's ultimately what you have to find out and learn: who am I? What's my message? What makes me truly authentic?

Master Your Voice

CONSCRICTION & FINDING YOUR NATURAL VOICE

My goal as a singer has always been to minimize bad tension and get rid of any constrictions that make singing harder than it needs to be. Achieving freedom and ease, taking off the pressure that causes strain and having an open and resonant sound that's pleasant and round is the goal. It has also been my goal as a vocal coach to teach my students how to get there, and an important element to reach that ideal goal is to respect the body and make it your ally instead of your enemy. Trusting that your body has infinite wisdom, basically, that of millions of years of evolution is something you may have to learn. Your body is sending you tiny little signals all the time, and you have to learn to interpret them so they can help you help your body operate at peak efficiency.

I see so many singers, beginners and professionals alike, who always seem to struggle with the sound of their voice, strain, constrictions, and tension in the wrong places. I have asked myself for years why that is, and the answer I came up with for myself is very profound: they just don't know how to listen to their bodies.

Your body wants to take care of you at any cost. The human body keeps itself running and thriving by continuing a number of processes that happen involuntarily. Your heartbeat to transport oxygen and nutrients, breathing transport oxygen inward and toxic waste products like carbon dioxide outward. You don't have to think about breathing since it happens involuntarily. You breathe when you sleep, and when you go for a run, you automatically breathe faster, and your heart rate speeds up to transport more oxygen through your body to help your muscles keep up with your desired pace.

Breathing is a matter of life and death, but it's also the thing we take for granted the most.

When you sing, your breath shouldn't be detached from the rest of your body. And it should be a flow that naturally leads to sound since the process of first inhaling air and then exhaling it through the vibrating vocal cords is what makes sound possible. In fact, without air, your vocal cords can't vibrate.

Singers often breathe either in a strained, detached way or very small and understated. Your breath should become part of the sound, much like it is part of the expression when you speak. Its intensity should represent the passage you sing: slow and liberal when you have a lot of time, quick and accented when you sing on a strong beat.

Try to imagine an actor speaking without hearing their breath. How would it sound if they were excited, sad, or angry and you didn't hear the sound of the breath reflect their emotions? Not only would it be stale and robotic, but it also wouldn't be very genuine, because the way the breath sounds very much reflects your intention.

Give yourself permission to breathe freely, not only out of necessity but because you want to include the natural sound of your breath and the way it makes your body feel.

Especially after having sung in choirs, singers tend to focus only on the pitches that need to be sung, and the breath is almost like a curse. It's not desirable to breathe at your individual pace since in a choir you need to blend in both in regards to the voice color and the way you breathe. As a soloist, however, you need to take a completely different approach. You're now an individual, not an entity.

Just like inhaling should be free, unconstricted, and deep, the way you exhale very much determines the way your voice sounds. The degree of tension (the good kind that comes from your support muscles) will also influence the degree of vocal cord closure. The amount of force you use to push the air towards and through the vocal cords determines how dense the tone will be. So, at times you will want to aim for a more breathy sound, which will use up a lot more air than a very focused and pure sound.

No matter what sound you intend to achieve, the way your breath flows, should at no time be constricted or forced. There should be a balance between the pressure that comes from the core and the degree of vocal cord closure. Too much pressure with a wide gap between vocal folds will create friction and strain. Too little pressure and your vocal folds will fail to vibrate.

Even as you hold a very long high pitch and apply the principle of "inalare la voce" (inhaling the voice), it should reflect the intention that precedes the technique. Inhaling the voice is, of course, not literally possible. Don't ever vocalize while inhaling, since it can cause damage. It's more about the feeling of holding your breath, controlling every bit of air that flows outward so that the perfect pressure, as well as the ideal amount of air, is exhaled in combination will vocal folds that are well closed, not too tight and not too loose. The higher the pitch, the less air should flow outward, since your vocal folds naturally come together tighter as you raise the pitch. Once you reach the very top, especially in head voice, there is a sensation of almost holding your breath, since there's very little air that flows outward. Subglottal pressure (the pressure of the air below your vocal cords) increases with higher pitches, and it's very much a matter of training to achieve very tight cord closure to get that perfectly resonant tone without a trace of breathiness. Breathiness always indicates air that moves through your vocal folds which is not translated into pure pitch. You hear the sound of air escaping. This is sometimes desirable in pop music, but should only be practiced once you have a good sense of and control over the degree of vocal cord closure.

The meaning of the lyrics in a song also indicates the amount of physical work you should put into a phrase. When you're very tranquil and relaxed, your body will feel a lot different than at times when you feel angry or excited and can hardly contain yourself. Don't detach your voice from the rest of your body! Your voice is part of your body and all parts involved have to communicate in perfect harmony to achieve ease and minimize strain and constrictions. Your breath, your jaw, your tongue, your shoulders, your back, your neck, your soft palate, and your larynx all play a part in the quality of tone, so always make sure you use your whole instrument.

Learning to sustain the good kind of tension in the right places, such as your support muscles, soft palate, and vocal cords, while minimizing strain in the jaw, the neck, and the shoulders, will help you save energy so you can work hard where it really counts. Learn to relax those body parts that would have an adverse effect on your sound and stamina if they were tight and tense. Often, we engage parts of our bodies that we don't even need. Shifting the head forward only creates tension in the neck, which will cause a strained tone. Tension in the arms and shoulders also harms good resonance.

Use breathing as a natural process that isn't just a necessity, but which feels good and becomes part of the vocalizing process. Your body wants you to inhale and exhale, but it doesn't like to do it when you treat it as a constant struggle. Your mind has a massive effect on your body. I know that it's often a problem to make the air last as you sing through a long phrase. But rather than trying to make the air last longer by collapsing and pushing it out, try to take the approach of economizing: take control of the amount of breathiness you add to your tone, which means you should always do it purposefully.

If you do have issues with vocal cord closure and have breathiness you can't control, you need to address that issue before beginning a battle with your whole body because you're constantly out of breath, which causes so much more than a lack of control: bad posture because you try to squeeze out the last bit of air, shallow breathing and gasping, which just keeps you in a vicious cycle of never having enough air, and actually having less and less air as you progress through the song. Breathiness also causes a lot of unnecessary strain on your vocal cords, which makes you push more and more to achieve more resonance and volume. Breathiness will most likely also prevent any ping or twang, which are the frequencies that carry above the band or orchestra, again causing you to strain and push, even more, wearing out your vocal cords in the long run.

You see, the problems that come with constricted air flow are manifold.

Just like a flute or clarinet can't make a sound without air, the voice needs good air flow to exist. And if you want to achieve ease in your singing, controlling your breath flow is one of the first things you should focus on to gain full control.

Having full control over your breath not only affects your singing but will also have a positive effect on your everyday life. I have a lot of strength in my breath and support nowadays, which didn't only help me with childbirth, but in all kinds of different areas in my life. I've built strong muscles and reflexes that allow me to take deep breaths, slowly or quickly, and exhale in the most controlled way, while relaxing my jaw and anything else that isn't involved in the actual process of breathing and vocalizing.

Whenever I inflate a bunch of balloons for my daughter's birthday party, I don't get out of breath, since I know how to inhale and exhale with adequate pressure, without getting dizzy quickly. I also know how to inhale deeply and calmly even when I'm under a lot of pressure, which relaxes my whole body. Breathing shallowly causes a lot of tension in your body, which also has an effect on your mind. I'm very conscious of what is happening in my body at any time. I recognize breathing patterns that indicate tension and calm my whole body by purposefully breathing in a way that puts my body at ease and takes it out of alarm mode.

Especially when you are in a recording studio or on stage, you want to know some tools that calm your body. You know how it feels when your voice starts shaking because your body shakes. It's so wonderful to have control over your body even if you're nervous or strained. It comes with years of training, and you get better and better as you keep practicing good breathing so that it eventually becomes second nature. You can begin practicing this today. Inhale deeply over five counts, making sure your ribs expand all the way around. Then, hold your breath for five counts without closing the epiglottis. This will require you to engage your support muscles since otherwise your ribs collapse and your air escapes. Then tighten your lips and exhale with an even air flow, as slowly as possible.

Another kind of constraint we put on ourselves is just limiting ourselves to the idea of a specific sound because of the way someone else sounds or a voice color we adore in our favorite singer. We love that sound and want to sound the same. But we all have a unique voice. Find your own beauty, and you will love singing so much more. Trying to sound like someone else will only cause frustration.

THE EVOLUTION OF YOUR VOICE

The voice is a fascinating, ever-changing, always growing part of who you are as an individual. Not only is it part of our physiology, but also a big part of our psychology. It contains and expresses a vital part of our identity, and this identity is usually shaped very early in life.

Unlike any instrumentalist who was born without his instrument and only added it to his life at some point, you were born with your instrument. At first, you use it to express your needs to let your mother and caregivers know when you're uncomfortable, when you need to be held and fed, when you want to sleep, and when you need entertainment. You quickly learn that your voice has an effect on the people around you and begin to use it to communicate.

You hear other voices around you day after day, and you begin imitating the sounds others make. This is precisely where you begin forming habits in regards to your voice. You also start to hear other people sing: your mother, your father, your siblings, singers on the radio and on television. If you're lucky and have parents who love to sing just for enjoyment, you are most likely to develop a healthy relationship with your voice that makes you want to explore new sounds without any negative preconceptions. You just love to sing and do it in a very natural and uninhibited way. Unfortunately, it doesn't happen that way for everyone.

Some parents tell their children that the way they sing is wrong or that there's something wrong with their voice. Some communicate the general idea that singing loudly is embarrassing, or that you shouldn't sing at all, or that girls are supposed to sing high and soft, with a breathy tone. They may tell their kids that it sounds awful because it's off pitch, so you better shouldn't even try it. You begin being very self-conscious when it comes to singing and avoid it altogether, out of fear someone will ridicule or criticize you. Not once does anyone mention that it's fun just to sing together, even if it's not perfect, and that indeed you can learn to sing on pitch.

The voice is so much more personal than an instrument that you play and then put away. You live with your voice day and night, in sickness and health, until the day you die. It's a reflection of who you are. When someone tells you that you can't play the piano well, it feels a lot different than someone saying that you can't sing. Not being able to sing on pitch makes us feel inadequate and like something is wrong with us. It's like we yearn to have full control over that part of our body because everybody admires it so much when someone can sing well. There's just something about knowing how to control your voice that exudes confidence and competence.

The good news is: no matter what your history is - singing can be learned. It may take a long time and a lot of effort, depending on your musical background, physical shape, learning style, discipline, tenacity, and how easily you connect with your body and emotions, but it can definitely be learned. In all my years as a voice teacher, I haven't had a single student who didn't improve dramatically with consistent practice and guidance. It definitely will not happen overnight, but with enough patience, grit, positive attitude, courage, commitment, and yes - TIME - you will be able to shape your voice into the best instrument you can possibly have. It will be with you at all times, and it's only up to you to bring out its full potential.

The journey will never end, no matter how advanced you become, how sound your technique gets, and how fancy you can adlib and improvise. Even some of the most successful singers still have vocal coaches after being in business for many, many years. The good singers know that they always need someone to check in with who can judge from the outside. We all need to brush up on our technique from time to time, so our voices can still do the hard work required for years of high pitches to come.

Besides, your voice never stops changing and continues to develop. It's so fascinating how dynamic it is. I've noticed that my voice has changed quite a bit over the years. And since I have always paid attention to sound and healthy technique, I can say that it has only changed for the better. I have gained strength, endurance, depth, and have a lot more brilliant resonance in my voice than I did 20 years ago. My continuous training hasn't only affected my singing voice, but also my speaking voice. I have almost perfect control and can use it in any way I want. That is so cool! There's just something about a warm and bright voice in combination with excellent diction and pitch control that seems to have a magic effect on people. Add musicality and feeling, and you will win over your audience any day.

Let me just tell you a little about my journey with my own voice. I was very blessed to be born into a family where singing was part of the normal everyday life. My dad was on stage as a singer while my mom accompanied him on the guitar or the accordion. My mom always sang with me and taught me easy little songs. Our family always sang for special occasions such as birthdays and Christmas. There was no judgment in regards to the way I sang, but my dad was officially the professional singer in the family.

I always knew I could sing. I remember singing harmonies with my mom when I was in kindergarten and having a lot of fun singing together. I went to a catholic day care, and we always sang a lot there, too. My mom always told me that I had a beautiful voice and singing was just part of everyday life. She wasn't a great singer, but she could sing the right pitches. I wouldn't have liked a fancy way of singing, but I did love a very straight forward way of just singing a straight forward melody and harmony. I didn't think much about how I sang, but just paid attention to the pitch accuracy and rhythm and understood how to make a song sound right.

I always had access to a piano and started plunking around early on, maybe at age 4 or 5. I figured out some melodies by trial and error and was fascinated with the sound that came out of the instrument when I played. It was an old piano, and I could already hear which keys were not tuned well. I just played it by ear and sang along. My mom showed me how to play a few very easy pieces, but never negatively criticized me. She was always happy to hear me make music just for the sake of fun. I think that's why I always just sang without overthinking too much. I just did it. It was natural. It was just part of life.

Everybody in my family did it, and we also did it together. We listened to a lot of classical music at home, so I also heard orchestras and opera singers. My parents never listened to pop music. Already then, I didn't like singers who had a very wide and wobbly vibrato but loved those singers most who had a more natural, clear, and bright sound in their voices. By the way, I've noticed over the years that kids generally love natural, friendly voices, which is caused by our natural disposition to perceive bright and high voices as loving and kind as opposed to dark and low voices that can sound more serious. No matter what someone's voice type may be, whenever the voice sounds very darkened and misplaced, it's not something we are naturally drawn to. Those voices that we love despite their darkness still have a natural sound to them. Have your parents ever pretended to sound like a monster? They would most likely have done that by darkening and lowering their voice.

Listening to the opera singers on stage, I was amazed at the virtuosity and ease they displayed and perceived this as a very desirable and admirable way to sing. Whenever my mom took me along to one of her jobs playing in the orchestra, I sat beside her in the orchestra pit and felt like I was in a world of magic when the orchestra began to play the overture. I had chills, it was so overwhelming. It's so different than listening to a recording because you can literally feel the vibrations of the double basses and timpani. When we came home afterward, I loved to disappear into my room the next day to play opera. I pretended to be an opera singer and imitated the way the soprano had sung, acted out the scene, and put on my mom's skirts. I imitated the soprano voice, including vibrato, portamento, and even attempted to sing in Italian by making up words that sounded like Italian.

Of course, I didn't know a single word of Italian. Since I only did this when I knew no one was listening, no one criticized me or told me how to do it. I just copied what I had seen and heard. I did not want anyone to see me do this, because I felt like they may think I was being ridiculous. In hindsight, maybe I was afraid of getting praise. I was actually pretty good at it, but wouldn't admit to anyone that I could sing differently from the way I sang in the children's songs we sang together as a family. Maybe it was the fact that my dad was supposed to be the expert, and he also sang some opera arias and everyone admired him for that. It was his role to be the singer, and I preferred to stay in the background. Maybe it was because I was such a shy child. I would have died if I had had to perform in front of someone as a singer. The piano was different, the voice was just so much more personal.

On the other hand, my dad was a singer who sang in numerous genres: classical, Schlager, and Volksmusik, which are very popular in Germany. I watched him on stage and in the recording studio, and he had quite a few appearances on television and the radio. This was normal everyday life for me. We knew some Germany celebrities, and it was normal to have famous people over at our house. I already sang in different styles, too, because I just imitated what was going on around me. I sang in chest voice and head voice and already knew that there was a difference, but at the same time, I didn't really think of the technical aspects as much as the sound I tried to imitate. I just knew how to create a sound that I had heard. I never had a very loud or strong voice, but always accurate in pitch with good breath control, as those were the things that I paid most attention to. I joined a kid's choir and had an occasional appearance with my parents singing in the background.

I never had any voice lessons as a child. As a matter of fact, I had my first voice lesson at age 25, when I began to study for my vocal performance degree at university. You may wonder how it is possible to become a professional singer without having any formal voice training before college. It only took about 2 years of college for me to begin making pretty good money with my singing skills. I also got the lead role in an opera production after having had only two and a half years of voice lessons.

The key to my quick progress was the fact that I had been musically trained from my childhood on. Not specifically my voice, but I had taken piano lessons since age six, and later studied the flute for a few years and even went to the conservatory to become a professional flutist. Even to this day, I find I have an advantage over many other singers since I understand music and know the ins and outs of different styles, which helps me sing smarter, not harder and be more expressive.

I know it's the main reason why I made rapid progress in my vocal studies. My ear had been trained from an early age, which is a considerable advantage at any time. I always notice that many singers know how to sing and control their voices, but are not able to communicate with other musicians due to a lack of experience. They often don't know how to differentiate between genres or how to be true to the musical style and use many different voice colors to be more expressive.

Knowing how to play an instrument will make it so much easier to learn new music since you don't always have to depend on someone else demonstrating. Listening to the original recording has the disadvantage that the sound of that singer gets stuck in your head and you most likely don't get as creative in regards to your own way of expressiveness. It's wonderful to explore new music all by yourself and hearing it for the first time as you sing and play it. I can't tell you how much fun it is to open up a songbook and just start playing a song I have never heard before. I get my very own ideas of how it could sound in my voice by giving the words meaning, as well as giving the harmonies and melody a purpose. It becomes my very own creation and feels like it's something entirely new and fresh.

If you don't play any instruments and think it may be too late in life to begin, I'm here to tell you that it's never too late. I could tell you numerous stories of students who started playing the guitar or the piano in their 50s, 60s, and even 70s, after taking voice lessons with me for a while, and how much that positively impacted their singing. They gained more confidence, more musicality, a new understanding of all the possibilities in music. They also trained their musician brain and coordination by practicing to play and sing at the same time. With practice, you can become a self-sufficient musician, a one-man or one-woman show who depends on no one else to make a polished performance happen. You can sing and play at your own tempo and choose your dynamic range on the fly. This is sometimes very helpful when you need to react to your surroundings. Playing at a bar with only two guests requires you to turn down intensity so there can still be a conversation.

On the other hand, when the bar is bursting at its seems, you better turn up the volume and overall intensity. The scenario can sometimes change within minutes. You also can change your set list around at a whim. Whenever I feel like I need a little break for my voice, I can pull out a Bill Withers song that's groovy yet easy on the voice. Yes, it does take a lot of training to become a solo show, but within a couple of years, you could take your skills to a whole new level - if you're consistent.

Among musicians, there's often a somewhat negative opinion about singers. Many singers don't know how to read music or any musical terms to communicate what's happening in the music, and also don't understand the lingo whenever an instrumentalist explains how to perform parts of the music. There are a lot of divas, both male and female, who act like they're the center of the universe and have little understanding for the fact that music isn't only an art but also a craft. Some are constantly concerned about their voice, can't sing out loud because they happen to have a phlegmy day or are on the verge of a cold. They can't talk before a gig, don't eat, drink only tea and generally have special needs. Granted that all of these behaviors have valid reasons, there are still many singers who are a lot of work to be around. I believe that as a singer you should continually educate yourself about your instrument as well as musical styles and theory. Playing an instrument will help you gain instant respect among your colleagues.

Be careful not to become one of those singers who constantly makes a big deal about singing. Be approachable, open, and knowledgeable - and do your homework. Unless you can sight read sheet music, you need to have studied your songs. And you should always memorize your music and lyrics as quickly as possible. I've always tried my best to convince colleagues that a singer can be an awesome musician too, and I think I have been successful in changing some of their negative opinions about singers.

My voice has continued to change throughout my entire life. Of course, the transition from my voice as a child to my adult voice may have been the most significant and noticeable. However, I can honestly say that as the changes were gradually happening, I didn't even realize anything was different.

I just knew how to sing, and even the changes in my voice didn't effect the way I sang. I just kept doing what I had always done, and my voice continued to work without any major problems. I think that not overthinking and being able to relax while singing played a big role in my success as a singer. I didn't stress out over small or even big things that didn't work. Whenever a high note was strained or cracked, I smiled and tried again.

I experimented with different registers, transitions, voice colors, dynamic levels, and phrasing to find out how to solve the problem. This is probably why I've learned so much about the voice. I just tried anything and everything that's possible with my voice, as long as it felt healthy. I always knew when I used an unhealthy technique, and I avoided to do these things. I love clear and clean tones in the voice, so that was always my goal. There are certainly genres that require a more raspy tone, but I strongly believe that the most healthy and efficient way to sing for the rest of your life is to aim for a clean and bright tone.

As I began taking voice lessons, I started studying very demanding repertoire, mostly in opera and classical music. Strong high pitches, coloratura arias, long phrases, floaty pianissimo high pitches, and in opera productions I was doing all of this while running and jumping around on stage, sometimes out of breath from all of the acting and commotion. It's amazing what some stage directors will come up with. You think, „I can't even do it without singing. And how exactly am I supposed to sing that E6 while hanging head down from the couch?" I guess this was all good training that prepared me to sing in even the most awkward situations.

I began to realize how important it was to revisit the basics and get them right: support, posture, breathing, resonance. I had to learn to keep my technique in place no matter what position my body was in. My voice continued to gain strength and stamina. I sang mainly opera for several years, which really trained my head voice in an athletic way. However, I was still writing my own songs at that time and had little recording sessions singing in chest voice. I was always more than a singer. I was a creator, a song writer, a musician.

I also sang in church and was leading the praise and worship team for a while. Playing the piano helped me conduct the band and keep things together. Of course, I sang mainly in chest voice there, too.

Years later, when I seriously began gigging with a party band every weekend, I remember my chest voice being strong up to a B-flat 4, but beyond that I had to switch into head voice. I was good at transitioning, but wasn't happy with the fact that I had to switch, since most pop and rock songs need that more gritty sound that head voice can't provide. Plus, it's much easier to stay in chest voice throughout the song instead of constantly having to transition.

When I finally decided that life as an opera singer wasn't for me, I went all in to perfect my belting technique. I still did freelancing work singing classical repertoire, but my main focus had shifted. After all, I wanted to be happy AND make a good living.

As I kept doing gigs with the band and less classical and opera singing, my voice became stronger singing high chest voice. I sang a lot. Sometimes I traveled all over Europe, flying from an opera masterclass in Denmark to a musical theater rehearsal in Prague, on to the performance in front of 3000 people in Vienna, and the next morning flying to Hanover to sing with the Federal Police Orchestra for a big celebration in a gigantic cathedral. I also remember being very sick one week, and having to sing through a few performances with a bad cold. I did my best, focused on great technique and the basics, and somehow always was able to deliver without hurting my voice. I can attribute this to a great technical foundation, but most of all knowing where my limits are. Of course, I was always very aware of what I did vocally so I wouldn't damage anything. I went to see a doctor to look at my throat to make sure I wasn't going to do any harm to my voice. Lots of gargling and intentional minimal warm-ups helped a lot.

All of this singing, the high demands, and the continuous practicing, made my voice so much stronger. I also believe that my voice color has changed quite a bit over the past twenty years. Thinking back, my voice wasn't nearly as strong and voluminous as it is today, although I still don't have a big voice per se. Changes in voice will always be part of your life as a singer, but when you have a solid technique, it can only change for the better. It will gain strength and depth instead of getting worn out and rough.

YOU'VE GOT THE POWER

It's a common misconception that singing high is harder than singing low. That may be true in regards to general body engagement and the amount of support you need that is coming from your core. However, there's even more of a limit in regards to how low you can sing in comparison to training to sing higher. Actually, training to sing higher is very much part of the process of becoming a more proficient and versatile singer.

The limitations you currently experience, are probably not the absolute limit of what you may be capable of doing in the future. It's possible to build up more power, stretch those vocal cords just a little bit more, and to slowly gain and master more pitches on the top, whereas on the low end of your voice, there's a very defined limit. Singing low means to bring your vocal cords into the shortest, most relaxed position possible while still allowing them to vibrate. After you achieve maximum shortness and thickness, you can't go any further.

You can practice controlling the lower pitches better, focusing on even breath flow and easing up on the pressure. That's why it is so hard to sing low and still have perfect control. As the gap between your vocal cords widens, more and more air passes through them, making control over long phrases even more difficult. It's so important always to keep your support on alert, even when you have rests or breaks, or sing lower. You want to hold on to that air as much as possible and send it through those vocal folds in a very controlled and steady manner, without letting it escape all too quickly. This will also prevent too much breathiness, which over long periods will make your cords tired. The most common pitfall when singing low is excessive darkening, lowering the larynx, and pressing too much in an attempt to achieve more volume.

Still, most singers feel like they struggle most on the high end. And they do feel like there is an end to their range. This is probably mainly owed to the break that naturally occurs between the two main registers of the voice and also that with more pushing the high pitches are literally choked off as the throat gets narrow. The break between registers will always be a reality for every singer. While it will never disappear, you can learn to sing through it and around it in a very smart and controlled way. The break doesn't have to be noticeable. Being aware of the minute differences in voice colors (brighter or darker) and the amount of weight (heavy or light) to bridge the gap between the two registers is key.

When working on singing higher with more power and less breathiness - which creates more strain on your vocal folds than a tone produced by well-closed vocal folds - you have to minimize any type of constrictions. You also should keep your voice in motion, just like your body naturally wants to be in movement.

Have you ever noticed that even when you think you are lying down still, your body is never static? You inhale and exhale, which makes your chest rise and fall, your heart beats, and if you did try to be entirely static, you would get experience some pain in some places, like your back, your neck, or your hips. Standing or sitting in the same position for a long time causes strain. That's why people who are paralyzed or lay in bed for an extended period, have to be turned every few hours. Even in your sleep, your body is very active. You turn without consciously doing it. You may even talk. Your brain never stops thinking, so you dream to make sense of all the fragments of experiences that are driving down the highway of your synapses.

Your voice doesn't like to be static either. Your vocal cords don't want to be locked into one position for a long time as they vocalize, because it strains them. Your larynx wants to move naturally, just like it does when you speak. You neither want to pull it up nor push it down over extended periods, but it should have the freedom to raise and lower as you speak or sing naturally.

When you are working on high and long pitches, you should give them a direction and a motion. Imagine a big concert hall, and you are throwing those sound waves to the far end where someone sits who is listening. Almost like a baseball. You want to give it speed and direction. You want to picture the pitch being thrown and flying toward your audience.

You also want to give your breath and air stream a direction and density. The higher and denser you want your sound to be, the more focus and density you will have to give to the air stream that passes through the vocal cords and is translated into the vibration that creates the pitch. You want it to be very compressed and focused, like a laser beam. Narrow and dense, so you have a lot of power, just like a laser beam can cut through tissue in surgery.

This requires you to keep everything in the place it needs to be without becoming static. Being static is something that your body will always fight against, so try to help your body do what it wants to do naturally.

Even when you belt high pitches and feel a lot of strain in your body, you should not stay in that same position, but look for a position to move to that will take off the strain. Alternating between denseness and short moments of relaxation will save your voice and make it possible to sing repertoire that takes a lot of power and strength physically.

Look for even the briefest moments of rest, moments to have a bit less tight vocal cord closure, a little more or less brightness, moving your larynx up or down for just a moment to express what the lyrics want you to communicate, bringing in a short moment of vocal fry for the onset if the lyrics need you to express that emotion of more passion or despair. The only way I can make it through exhausting sets is keeping in the variety so that I don't get too static in my voice color. It also makes it so much more interesting for your audience. Being bombarded by hours of the same voice color and intensity level gets very tiring.

But even when you hold a long pitch that you don't want to change in its sound, always imagine a point of arrival that you're running towards. Hold the pitch, but imagine it moving forward and upward. It will help you keep that arch of good tension to stay on pitch without getting tight in your throat.

I always do an exercise with my students which requires them to hold a long pitch, but sing a half step down and come back up as they hold it every second or so. Then they go back to holding that same pitch without alternating down and up but imagine doing the moving pitches. It does wonders each and every time, as it helps you to hold the tension without getting tense. Just thinking about the pitch moving will keep your soft palate lifted, your throat open, and your larynx dynamic.

So, next time you feel strain creeping in, try these techniques and remember to let your body do what it does best: breathe and flow.

HOW SINGING WILL CHANGE YOU

If you had known me when I was a child, you would have never guessed that I would turn out to be as confident as I am today. And I mean this in the most positive way.

This was me as a child: very shy, introverted, timid, never contradicting an adult, often terrified to speak up. Part of this was owed to the fact that my family life was very difficult. My dad had some serious issues with alcohol and was emotionally abusive, and I remember crying just about every day. Life felt heavy and difficult, but also amazingly wonderful when I escaped from reality by playing on the piano or singing. I began writing poems and songs early in life, because it beamed me into another world and really helped me cope with my dad telling me I'm useless. I always knew that I was different, but in a very positive and encouraging way. I felt like I was born for a higher purpose.

I was the type of child who had a very vivid imagination and could think up the most awesome stories. But I was very shy when it came to meeting new people. Even when I got older, I was a rather shy person. I was mortified of making a phone call to an office, and I always avoided expressing any complaints. I just went with the flow and hated going against what everybody else did. I let people run over me, just because I wanted to please everybody. I just was afraid to stand up for myself, because I was scared of rejection. I was never with the popular crowd in school, and I was even scared to raise my hand in class. I was just so afraid of not being liked.

When I think back, I remember exactly the way I felt when I was told I did something wrong. I just froze up and thought it was the end of the world. It cut so deep. I think this is why I always wanted to show everyone that I had so much more in me and that one day I could stand up and show how great I am.

Knowing me now, you would never guess that was me. Who am I nowadays? I'm confident, have a strong opinion, stand up for myself, won't let other people's opinions influence me to where they make me doubt everything I stand for. I love constructive criticism and take to heart what I'm told, but won't let someone's negativity disrupt my day. I'm not afraid anymore to say something that someone won't agree with. I will start up a conversation at gatherings where I don't know anyone, approach anyone I want to talk to in public places, make inconvenient phone calls with ease, and stand up for what I believe, even if everyone around me has a different opinion. I don't shy away from confrontations if they're necessary.

You may ask how it is possible to morph from being a total introvert into someone with self-confidence. I'm convinced that I owe almost everything to my experience as a performing artist and my life on stage. The many, many hours I spent on stage, performing and singing for people who were essentially strangers, as well as those who are very close to me, has fundamentally changed the way I deal with people and situations.

I even remember when I began studying voice at university, that we had studio class once a week, and everyone had to get up in front of the class to perform a piece they'd been working on. There was the challenge of memorizing the lyrics, getting the melody and phrasing right, counting correctly, and getting the entrances right, all while paying attention to the accompanist and acting out the character. It was so incredibly difficult for me to act. It was easy to feel the song, but to actually show it through my gestures and expressions seemed awkward as soon as someone was watching me. I knew what I wanted to do, but somehow I just froze up and couldn't move my arms the way I could when I practiced alone. It was like watching myself from the outside, constantly thinking about how stupid I looked and not daring to take any risks.

As I gained more and more experience, I began to take more risks, because I learned that nothing terrible would happen if I just dared to gesture a little bit more with my arms and body. Slowly, very slowly my confidence grew. As almost everything that could go wrong did go wrong at one point or another at least once, I learned that people still loved my performance and often didn't even notice that something had not gone the way I had intended it. Always remember that only you know what you intend to do. To your audience everything may still sound and look perfect, even if it didn't exactly go the way you had intended.

By now, I can get up on any stage in front of any audience and sing, but I also apply all of this confidence in me to my daily life. Singing has taught me better posture and better breathing, which makes me stand up straighter and stay calmer in stressful situations. I believe that even giving birth to my daughter was affected positively by the breathing technique I learned in singing. I kept my jaw relaxed while breathing in a very controlled and non-stressed way. The midwife told me that that helped the process immensely since the pelvic musculature is connected to the jaw musculature. When you strain your jaw, the pelvic floor gets tense and doesn't allow for the baby to slide down the birth canal easily. I did have a pretty smooth delivery, so I guess singing slow descending scales during labor didn't hurt.

I had wondered if my neighbors had noticed that I had sung and given birth, but when I showed them the baby the next day, they were totally surprised because they said they hadn't heard anything. I remember that I focused on taking one deep breath as I felt each contraction coming, and then just relaxing my jaw and body as I began descending the scale from the first high pitch. By the time I arrived at the lowest pitch in my voice, the contraction had passed.

I notice that I generally breathe more deeply nowadays when I face stress, and that helps me to stay calm and grounded as well as keep tension away from my shoulders and neck. You know how your body just gets tense and stiff when you stress, and that causes headaches and all kinds of little pains of aches. I haven't had any headaches or jaw tension for several years. Being on stage is always somewhat stressful on your mind and body.

Having trained those stressful situations for almost twenty years as a professional performer has taught my subconscious mind that it's a routine situation and will always pass without negative consequences. On the contrary! I've conditioned my mind that those stressful situations will always result in a reward: applause, compliments, getting paid (what a nice reward!), follow up bookings (and more money!), happy faces, raving reviews, and most importantly, a sense of accomplishment. It's just such a great feeling to do something that's scary and make it through.

Getting up on stage not only becomes something to look forward to but almost starts acting like a drug you always want more of, which can partially be explained by the chemicals your body releases when you are the center of attention, and everyone is watching you. The adrenalin always kicks in and blows away any tiredness, so it is definitely like a drug. After a big performance, you always feel like there's a void, and you want more of the experience. Applause is something you have to learn to accept and appreciate since it can be hard to handle when you're not used to it. But once you have learned to receive it, you will crave it.

We're all taught to be modest and not to be too vain. It's quite a process to come to the realization that it's not a negative thing to believe in one's own greatness. It's the best feeling in the world to know you've made someone happy with your performance, and having touched someone even just for a moment is very rewarding.

If you're a shy and introverted person and think you can never be a great performer because you're simply terrified to get on stage and you feel like you can't be yourself when everyone has their eyes glued on you: be assured that all of this can change, and you can use your introverted personality to your advantage as an artist, because you can combine your inner world that's filled with tons of imagination and emotion, with the skill to share it with other human beings, who by the way, feel or have felt these same emotions.

Being a singer is different from being any other type of musician since you have not only melodies and harmonies to express yourself, but also the wonderful gift of language to tell everyone what's on your heart and mind. The act of constantly memorizing lyrics will train your brain to begin remembering language by engraving sounds and pictures into your memory, the effects of which you will also notice in everyday life. You start to appreciate the beauty of words and the emotions they evoke.

MAKING THE REGISTERS WORK FOR YOU

This is probably the greatest struggle for every singer, no matter what genre, age, level of experience, gender, or training background. Your vocal registers are your basic tools in creating sound, and yet there's so much misunderstanding and confusion about them.

In this chapter, I want to simplify and demystify all you may have heard about the registers.

Basically, there are two mechanisms in the human voice: the heavy mechanism and the light mechanism.

In the heavy mechanism, the large mass of your vocal cords is moved and vibrates. Both the muscle tissue and the membrane tissue that the vocal cords consist of are at work, which creates a thick and full sound. You employ this mechanism most of the time when you speak or shout. Singing in this heavy mechanism will feel like slowed down speaking or controlled shouting, depending on the intended intensity level. When you talk to someone who is right in front of you, you will not have to be very loud, so you don't have to create very tight vocal cord closure to sustain the sound in chest voice without breaking or flipping. The further that person you're talking to moves away from you, the more you will have to raise your voice both in pitch and in intensity for them to still hear you well and understand your words. You have to work harder on enunciating and making all the sounds resonate, so the sound actually travels a bit further.

Once you picture them on the other side of a large parking lot, you will have to work a lot harder for them to hear you. You could compare this to what's commonly described as belting. Have you ever tried to communicate with someone who's on the other side of a parking lot? Do you remember that you had to make consonants extra hard and vowels extremely open to have a chance to be understood?

Even when you talk every day, you use your heavy chest mechanism for the most part.

On the other hand, the light mechanism is not used as much in your everyday use of your voice. If you screeched like a little girl because there's an immediate danger, you would most likely use your head voice if you're a woman. Although men don't use this mechanism as much in their speech, they still can use it the same way a woman can.

As far as the voice is concerned, men and women essentially have the same parts built in. It's only because boys are taught to sound like men that they usually have a harder time accessing this register. Not only the actual pitch and how high or low it is determines the register used, but much more the actual way you want to sound. You could take the screeching sound down a whole lot in pitch and still be in head voice. You could also yell from the top of your lungs at a really high pitch without breaking into head voice.

Without going into too many technical terms, I would still like to point out what the fundamental differences between those two registers are. This will help you understand them better and also give you a visual image of what's happening at any given point of time in your singing.

When you sing, the vocal folds close, which increases air pressure right below your vocal cords. This is called subglottal pressure. This increased pressure causes the vocal folds to open, creating an oval-shaped gap between them, which releases the pressure in the trachea. This process repeats in sequence very quickly, creating a glottal vibration, e.g., in the vocal folds. This is also referred to as a glottal cycle. There are mainly three layers the vocal folds consist of. Muscle tissue, ligament or membrane tissue, and mucous. When employing chest voice, the larger mass of the whole vocal folds in a somewhat thickened state is vibrating, creating a rather full sound that resonates mainly in the chest area. You can easily feel these chest vibrations by placing your hand on your chest as you speak in a very normal every-day voice. The muscles that are responsible for keeping the vocal folds in the heavy mechanism are the arytenoids.

In my years of experience with my voice students, I've learned that there are many singers, usually women, who have a hard time accessing their chest voice when they sing. Although there are rare cases in which they haven't even learned to use their chest voice when they speak by having gotten into the habit of speaking very lightly and high-pitched as children already, most women have no difficulties speaking in their chest voice. But as soon as they begin to sing, they slip right into head voice. It's such a hard habit to break. Once you start imitating certain sounds early in life, you just go on autopilot. If that means automatically singing in head voice, it will be a big undertaking to gain ease in your chest voice singing.

After having done quite a bit of research on my own students by asking them about their singing and speaking habits in the past as well as talking to speech therapists and their experiences with individuals who have vocal problems or damage, it is very clear that many girls already begin to imitate a very heady sound, because it sounds more feminine. They want their voices to be perceived as light, bright, and high - very much in contrast to a masculine voice which is perceived as darker, heavier and lower. When these girls and, later, women join a choir, they usually sing soprano, which means they mostly sing higher pitches, which are indeed easier to sing in head voice. This would all be great if the chest voice were not neglected entirely. But unfortunately, this is the case for so many female singers. A boy who has a high and bright voice and sings the higher parts all the time may develop much of the same problems and later have problems trying to achieve a very chesty and robust sound.

However, for male singers, the problem is usually the opposite. Often times they don't ever sing in head voice and don't know how to access it. This drastically limits the vocal range, since chest voice has a definite limit on the top before it needs to transition into head mechanism, which can expand the range by far more than an octave, adding on to the range of mere chest mechanism.

Knowing all of your registers and having full control over them, will give you the freedom to express exactly what you want to convey with the voice color of your choice, but much more importantly it will help you sing through the passaggio in a way that makes sense and enables you to stay in control. No involuntary flips or breaks, no pitch slipping away and causing inaccurate intonation.

The last thing you want to happen is to break into head voice too soon when you're singing a power ballad. The climax is just about to build, and you want to belt out that high pitch, but then you have to break into head voice, which will make for an entirely different sound. It just isn't the right thing in every case, since you want that more gritty and full sound. Head voice just has an inherently different sound quality than chest voice. If you always switch into head voice when the pitches get higher, it will sound to your audience like you're taking the easy route and obviously can't sing with that much power at the top of your range. It definitely is a lot more demanding to belt out that high pitch without breaking into head voice, and it takes a lot of training to sound controlled, but it's also the way that brings across the most credibility when you sing about things that have an extremely high urgency. I think some parts of songs need to be sung as if your life depends on it. At least, that's what needs to come across.

Think of the chorus of „It's Raining Men" being sung in a head voice. Head voice isn't exactly what is expected. Of course, if you changed the instrumentation and arrangement, you could make a „soft" version out of the song, but if you want to bring across that power and determination that's in the song, you just have to belt it out in chest or mixed voice with a chest heavy resonance.

If you just casually sing that climax like it doesn't really matter to you, your audience will be disappointed about your lack of commitment to the meaning and urgency. They won't believe you when you sing about life and death like you're on coffee break. When what you sing about is truly urgent like you want to shout it from the rooftops, you need to put in that much work to create that sound. There's just a different kind of urgency in chest voice since it's the sound you use every day in your speaking voice. And seriously: when you shout from the rooftops, you would actually shout, which would be very chesty. Have you ever tried to shout at someone in head voice? It would sound funny.

Head voice is meant for the really high stuff, the more classical music, and for a more artsy sound. In pop music, it's used sparingly and differently than in other genres.

Even in head voice, there are many different colors you can sing. It can sound full and very obviously heady with lots of space between your larynx and vocal cords, lots of pharyngeal space, very highly lifted soft palate. But there's also the option to sound less full and classical and instead very bright, light and sensitive. Head voice will also give you the option to get into falsetto, which is a more breathy sound in head voice.

Everything I've just elaborated on is my own version of explaining the registers. Even among vocal coaches around the world, there's no consensus as to how many registers there are, how they are produced, and what they are named. Some talk of up to eight passaggi or transition areas in your voice.

The most important thing about all of this is that it has to make sense to you and that it should help you sing better by understanding how many different sounds your voice can make and how to do this deliberately.

You should never neglect any of your registers or any part of your range in any register. To give your vocal folds and the surrounding muscles the best workout, you need to make sure you always warm up through all of the registers, singing both low and high, loud and soft. In my opinion, every singer should sing different genres from time to time, because it's good practice and expands your repertoire of what's possible vocally.

Singing classically has a lot of advantages and will train you in different ways than just singing jazz or pop. Classical music demands a high degree of accuracy, perfect articulation and resonance. Popular music, on the other hand, gives you a lot more freedom as to how you can express the music. There's room for improvisation and changing details here and there such as changing or adding pitches, timing, rhythmic variations, and voice color.

Every genre has its own set of rules when it comes to technique and sound quality. You want to expand your toolbox continuously so you can master more and more sound qualities and colors. That way you will almost never experience any limitations to express yourself with your voice because you're not missing a whole array of techniques that you've never explored. I always hear the difference when I listen to musical theater singers who are classically trained and those who aren't. The classically trained singers have so much more accuracy and control because they have learned the basics so well. It usually sounds so much more refined and controlled. The most outstanding pop singers do have some classical training and continuously get coached to get feedback on any bad habits that may have crept in.

On the other hand, some classical singers have never learned to sing popular music in a more vocally relaxed way. Since they need not project when a microphone is used, the sound should be more intimate often times and should reflect a natural speaking tone rather than something artistic and virtuosic. You just can't sing „One Moment In Time" with full classical head voice. If you did, it would just sound wrong and over the top.

One common misconception about singing is that the higher you sing, the more air you will need. While the sub-glottal air pressure does increase as you sing higher, less air flows through the vocal folds. The higher the pitch, the tighter the folds close and the smaller the gap between them becomes, creating a higher frequency with a faster-moving glottal cycle.

Whenever I sing very high pitches in head voice, it almost feels like holding my breath, since very little air moves through my vocal cords. There's a great but lengthy cadenza at the end of the famous aria "Caro Nome" from Verdi's Rigoletto. Whenever I sing it, I'm totally out of breath after I get through. Not because I'm out of air, but because I'm hardly exhaling any air at all. It's really high, and the pitches are held at a pianissimo dynamic marking for several seconds. I inhale deeply but never get to fully exhale for a long time, making it feel like I'm just holding my breath forever, like going on a dive. This sensation is often described as "Inalare La Voce" (Italian for "inhaling the voice") in the school of Bel Canto. You can apply this principle even to pitches that aren't extremely high. Just don't let a lot of air flow through your vocal cords if you want a very focused and non-breathy sound with a lot of overtones. Essentially, you have to master the art of using exactly the amount of air that's required to make the vocal folds vibrate at the pitch and dynamic level you desire. No more and no less.

You can achieve this by having consistent and continuous support from your core (around your ribs) while having really good and efficient vocal cord closure. Both of these elements can be trained separately at first, but putting them together creates true magic since you will have absolute control over the amount of air you let pass through your vocal folds as well as the intensity of your tone. It's wonderful to be able to adjust the level of breathiness or the absence thereof intentionally. These processes all require a high level of awareness as to what muscles control these processes.

It's like learning tennis. In the beginning, you would begin to swing the racket toward the ball that if flying in your direction. It's very likely that you won't even hit the ball because you don't have a good sense of the distance and speed of the ball and racket yet. You may entirely under- or overestimate the needed speed and direction you need to swing. The more you practice, the better you can coordinate eye and body, and as you gain experience, you can fine-tune better. In singing, it's all about executing over and over again. At first, you may not even hit the right pitch, but the more you practice, the better you will become at getting the details right.

Whenever you want to sing high with intensity, you need to make sure you have really good vocal cord closure, no matter what register you're singing in. Pushing a lot of air through the vocal folds while trying to achieve a loud tone is very straining because the air just creates a lot of friction on the cords. Whenever you feel scratchiness while you're singing high and loud, it's probably because you're letting too much air escape while having a wide gap between your vocal cords. You're pushing way too much air against them. This creates a vicious cycle: you run out of air quickly, so you keep gasping for air, never taking a deep and controlled breath. You compensate by leaning against your vocal cords even more since your support muscles are not making the air stream you push through your cords very dense. Again, not having the perfect combination of air pressure and cord closure will result in strain.

Even within a given register, there are many variations in tone quality you can create. In the heavy mechanism, you can mix in some head resonance, and in the head register, you can mix in chest resonance. Depending on how much you mix, you will be able to create any mix you desire, either more on the chest resonance or head resonance end. The mixed voice isn't a separate register, but rather a way to mix resonance without abruptly changing mechanisms. I know that this is where a lot of confusion persists.

Have you ever tried to sing in high chest voice by just

shouting out very loudly? This probably felt very uncomfortable and straining, because you relied only on the heavy mechanisms, while your body wants to naturally switch to a different position that will make it easier. Switching to head voice would take a lot of strain off your vocal cords, but of course, you don't want to sound full out heady when you are in the middle of the chorus in an upbeat rock song. So what do you do? You just lighten up a little and allow a little bit of head resonance, while keeping that tight vocal cord closure and without letting it tilt into head voice all the way.

This is a very difficult process and demands excellent control over both heavy and light mechanisms and the fine-tuning between them. You see, there's not only heavy or light. There are countless nuances between the two since it is possible to have a very fluent transition. The transition between chest and head register can be smooth instead of abrupt.

To practice this, you could begin singing a medium-high pitch in chest voice in a more heavy and dark mechanism, then gradually brighten up the color and lessening the chesty quality. You could also try to transition between registers while holding the pitch, so you get a feeling for that exact moment when it happens and how you actually control the switch. You could also experiment with how soft you can get in chest register without it tilting into full head voice, or even going higher to the next pitch without letting it suddenly flip into head voice, but instead making it seamless. The bottom line is: there will always be a break in your voice, but you can learn to control it. It takes a lot of practice, so if you're serious about becoming a great singer, you should put exercises that help you achieve this on your daily agenda.

The transition between the registers will always be an issue that occurs over and over again if you want to use the whole range of your voice. No matter how many years you have been singing, the passaggio is a natural part of your voice, and it will benefit you if you don't look at it as a problem but a friend you need to build a relationship with since you're stuck together for the rest of your life. You will get more and more skilled in every area of your voice, as long as you incorporate specifically targeted exercises into your daily warm-up routine. Learning to fine-tune the different placements and positions of all the parts involved in your voice to create the sound and color you desire is a true art and can only be achieved with a lot of repetition and experimenting.

If you're a pop singer, you should also want to master head voice and the transitions to and from it, and as a female classical singer, you should not leave out your chest voice. Done correctly, these are all part of your voice, and should be used.

Even if you don't use one of the registers as much as the other one, training both consistently is always excellent training for your voice and helps you to become much stronger and more coordinated. It will help you understand the passaggio or the area that connects the two registers. Just like working out only one body part won't help you have a balanced and strong body, only singing in one register will limit your possibilities drastically. If you lay in bed every day and only worked out your arms with heavy weights, the muscles in your legs would begin to shrink, and you would probably break a bone easily once you get up and try to jump down a chair. Strengthening your entire range, from the lowest to the highest pitch, will strengthen your voice overall.

We've talked about head voice and chest voice. But what

exactly is whistle register? You remember the way head voice works? It's called the light mechanism because less mass of the vocal cords vibrates. In whistle register, an even smaller area on the edges of your vocal folds vibrates. Less air passes through the folds, keeping them closed even tighter. The most important aspect of this mechanism is that it's not loud or pushed at all. It should actually feel very light, barely letting any air out, but at the same time feeling very relaxed in the throat.

Whistle register is actually an overtone that is created by just the edges of the vocal membrane vibrating. When you hold your breath and then slowly begin to let the tiniest amount of air out while softly vocalizing, you will create a very high tone. It may not be controllable at first and sound terrible, but if you pay attention to the pitch and try to stay close to the one that comes out the first moment, you can actually learn to control it more and more.

A lot of people have asked me if they can just do this while inhaling since it feels so much easier. Let me make my answer very clear: DO. NOT. EVER. VOCALIZE. WHILE. YOU. INHALE!!! This is unnatural and really bad for your vocal cords. The reason why it feels easier to create a whistle tone while inhaling is that it's easier to minimize airflow, which helps the very light and dense quality of a while tone being produced.

The way I practice the very highest frequencies my voice can possibly create, is by singing short high pitches and immediately sliding down. Think of a soft screech. Relax the jaw and keep it relaxed throughout the exercise, then inhale before singing a very light high pitch and move away from it right away to keep it all short and light. As it gets easier, you can slow down the exercise, so you stay on that very high pitch a little longer.

Remember, it should always feel light and comfortable. No pushing. No hoarseness. Just holding in the air as much as possible. Always be well warmed up before attempting this. If you get hoarse easily from doing this, you are pushing too hard and putting too much pressure on your vocal cords. The air stream is too massive and not laser-focused as it should be.

Let me say one more thing: don't attempt to go to the most challenging techniques without first having mastered the basics: good posture and support, controlled breathing (inhaling and exhaling), and minimizing bad tension in your body (jaw, neck, shoulders).

If you want to make sure that you have all the basics in place to build upon, you can check out my course „Back To The Basics" at www.masteryourvoice.tv

Just like you wouldn't just decide to compete in the Olympics as a runner next week without ever having trained, you also need to slowly work yourself up to your goals, step by step. It takes an athlete years of training to be one of the best in the world. If you think the voice is different, you're wrong. Your body is your instrument, and you need to have a training strategy to be able to take on more significant demands. Always remember that your instrument doesn't just consist of your vocal cords, but your whole body is involved, which is why your health and overall strength always play a vital role in your singing.

A problem that persists for many singers is knowing what register they are singing in at any given moment. Sometimes it's not clear if you're still in chest voice as you're going up the scale, while sometimes it may be absolutely obvious.

Master Your Voice

I find that the amount of vocal cord closure has a lot to do with this problem. If you have poor vocal cord closure, your chest voice will easily break into head voice without you experiencing an actual break. Breathiness is an indicator of muscles that are not fully engaged. Having a more breathy sound will usually promote a smooth transition between registers, but will also prevent you from staying in chest voice as you sing higher or in full head voice as you sing lower. Sometimes you absolutely need to remain in chest voice, for instance, if you want to sing a pop ballad that requires very intense and energetic top pitches that have a rich quality.

Vice versa, if you sing a classical soprano aria, you should not switch into chest voice, since this would not suit the style. The sound of your head voice is what's expected here. Also, classical technique is all about creating the perfect resonance that carries over an orchestra or other instruments without any amplification.

In Jazz, you could often utilize a variety of approaches, from heavier chest voice for a short moment to a very light and slightly breathy tone, but with very smooth transitions and dynamic changes.

What's important to keep in mind is that you should never think of the registers as something static or rigid. Head and chest resonances are often mixed to some extent, and there's a never-ending amount of variations to create different sounds with your register mechanisms as well as the amount of vocal cord closure, pharynx position, soft palate lift, tongue placement, etc. There's literally no other instrument in the world that has as many possibilities as the human voice.

To become a great performing artist, you have to learn how to use all of these tools to create an unending myriad of sounds in order to express all the emotional facets of the songs you sing. You must sharpen your blade every day to become more proficient in using these tools so you can create a perfect piece of art. I'm always overwhelmed when I hear a new voice that really touches me.

Although most people who listen to an artist will never know the technique behind the expressive sound, I always hear and see the connection between the artistry of the singer using their instrument and the connection to the song and the audience. Without technique, you will be very limited in your ways to express yourself with your voice, and without the emotional aspect and the connection to the music, all the great technique will not touch anyone. It's very frustrating to find that you can't do what you want to do because you haven't mastered that technique.

What makes us human is the unpredictability of our voice colors that can express every aspect of our complex emotions. That's why despite all of the advanced technology in the world, human beings will never be obsolete. There's a human aspect that can never be replicated, at least that's what I believe. Even random imperfections that may be calculated by algorithms would never be the same as genuine and authentic human emotions.

KEEPING YOUR INSTRUMENT AT PEAK EFFICIENCY

This is an area that is hugely neglected by a lot of singers. The coolest thing about being a singer is that you always have your instrument with you. You never have to carry any heavy cases, buy any special equipment, and don't have to clean it up after use. You never have to replace any parts, worry about the wood cracking when you go from cold outside temperatures to warm inside spaces or keep the room at 60-70 percent humidity. You never have to tune it or hire someone to transport it when you move to a new home. It's the most convenient instrument in the world. But it's also the most delicate and irreplaceable.

It will only work at its best if you take good care of yourself in every way. So, maybe you need to shift your mindset a little.

The problem that seems the most prevalent is the fact that the majority of human beings are not as in touch with their bodies as they could be. Since we don't live in harmony with nature's cycles any more but instead try to defy our biologically instilled needs it in many ways, it becomes harder to listen to our bodies' subtle hints and signals about its state of well-being.

What makes it even more complex is the fact that mind and body are very much connected. Your spiritual and mental balance is a prerequisite for a balanced body and vice versa.

Nowadays, we don't only ignore the many signals our body sends us, but we literally suppress its attempts to rebalance. Instead of resting, we drink coffee when we're tired. Instead of taking time off the screen, we pop a couple of Aspirins when we have a headache. When our nose is stopped up, we take Benadryl, instead of understanding that our body is trying to help by telling us that we need to slow down to let it do its job and fight against a cold virus. We stay up half the night working and stressing and wonder why we can't go to sleep as soon as we hit the sack. So we take a sleeping pill. We live against the natural cycles of our hormones which are linked to the cycle of day and night, summer and winter. We eat food that our body doesn't recognize as anything digestible and wonder why we have so many allergies. We hardly go outside anymore to breathe fresh air, because our homes and workplaces are air-conditioned and have the same temperature day and night, summer and winter.

We eat processed foods with added colors, preservatives, sugars, and flavors, and then take an arsenal of nutrition supplement pills to make sure we get vitamins and minerals. We eat more food and have more variety available to us than ever before in human history, but are getting more and more sick. Diabetes, thyroid disorder, allergies, acid reflux, Alzheimer's, obesity, anorexia, depression, and ADHD are at an all-time high, and more ailments are added to the list of common problems all the time. We get burned out to the point of having to be hospitalized. We don't have to do any more physical work, because we have cars, dishwashers, electric toothbrushes, smart home devices, and grocery delivery. We literally could live without ever getting up.

It looks like we have everything we need, but are not getting stronger and more resilient but instead weaker and less resistant to even a common cold. We get older but not healthier. We have immunizations against a lot of serious diseases, but more people die of strokes and heart attacks than ever before. We order a burger and fries with diet coke to save calories. We add artificial sweeteners instead of just getting used to less sweet tastes. Our body receives the signal „sweet," but there's no sugar. There are fat-free cheese and milk, and tons of „free of" foods and drinks, but we have more digestive irregularities and problems than ever before. Instead of eating half the portion size, we artificially reduce fat and sugar content.

We live in cities that are hustling and bustling day and night. There's no absolute darkness or quiet anywhere. We are exposed to constant stimuli and noise. We are surrounded by electronic devices that emit radiation constantly. We hardly have any moment in the day where we're just alone with our body and mind. The last thing we do before we sleep is look at a screen, and it's also the first thing we do in the morning.

I feel that as singers we need to learn again to listen to our body if we want to use it as the vessel and source of our craft. We can't expect our voices to work at their best if we neglect our bodies and just mute out all the subtle signals and signs it sends us.

We also need to take care of our mental health and learn to balance ourselves. We've all experienced what it's like to perform when we're emotionally out of balance. The voice is definitely affected by our feelings.

The way you live your life every day has an impact on the way your voice works. If you want your voice to perform like a top-notch athlete, you will have to live like one. You can't manage nervousness or become more confident when you're not connected to your inner self. Self-doubt arises from an imbalance and dissonance between who you truly are and the fear of what others may perceive about you.

We need to learn again to live our lives as closely as possible to the way it was originally intended to be lived. Healthy sleep and food are only the beginning. Human interaction, healthy relationships, and self-love are all part of who we were created to be.

I found that getting outside and being in nature every single day has improved my life not only in regards to my physical health but also my mental health. Meditating while I walk or run and taking in the beauty of nature with all of my senses, has given me a much more positive outlook on everything.

When I feel overwhelmed or stuck, I go for a walk in the forest. I'm so much more focused and productive after taking a break and allowing myself to put some space between me and the nitty gritty details of my work. It calms and grounds me, and it reminds me of the inevitability of the natural cycles of life. Instead of fighting against it, which is a fight that only leads to pain, I accept and honor my body, mind and spirit and the way they exist in time and space. I personally need 7 to 8 hours of sleep, and if I don't allow my body to rest and recharge enough, there are consequences. The brain can only operate at its best when we get enough sleep.

If I deny my body good food, there are unavoidable consequences. My body wants to work for me day and night, as long as I give it what it needs. It has infinite wisdom, but we need to let it do what it needs to do. My needs are genetically determined, so I need to have a positive attitude about giving my body all the things it needs. My concentration is best when I have been taking good care of my body and mind.

As humans, we are not only physical beings, but our spiritual well-being plays a massive role in our lives as well. Your body could be perfectly well, but just think of how you feel when you get some bad news: your mind significantly affects every other area of your being, including your body.

You can be totally energetic and motivated one moment, and completely crushed and incapacitated the next moment if your mind isn't in the right place. Your mind can affect your physical well-being, both in positive and negative ways. Our mind can literally make us sick or help us heal.

Our brain can only focus deeply and be creative when we don't put any obstacles in the way that impairs the miraculous capabilities of what's between our ears. Your brain has the capacity to do great things, expanding not only your knowledge but also shaping your personality.

If you've ever gone on YouTube and gotten lost watching those amazing videos that show the stunning things humans can do, you know that there are actually quite a few people in the world who do unbelievable things. Some play soccer with no feet, others memorize a whole phone book. Everyone has the same potential inside. Becoming a master is just a matter of lots and lots of repetition, unwavering focus and creating the best environment for your body and mind so it can be transformed into its best shape. Always remember what Henry Ford said: Whether you think you can or you can't - it's true! You are the one who creates your own reality every single day. Everything you do today has an effect on your future, and it's up to you what that future will look like. No matter how many times you have failed at something: the more you keep trying and repeating, the better you will get.

I can't tell you how many times I tried something for the first time and completely messed it up. Total failure! The first time I tried to play tennis: couldn't hit the ball. The first time I baked a cake all by myself: hard as a rock. The first time I tried an oil painting: the colors bled into each other, and it looked totally messy. But as I kept trying and trying, failing over and over again, I learned what mistakes to avoid as I continued to try different approaches until there was an improvement. I'm proud to say that I'm a pretty darn good baker today.

I remember creating my first web page. I didn't have any knowledge about how to go about it. I was a college student and had no money to pay someone to do it for me, so I had to figure it out myself. I went online and started looking for forums that were about creating websites. Some people had been doing it a lot longer than I had. I searched for threads that were about the specific problems I encountered. What encouraged me was the fact that I wasn't the only one who had those problems. I didn't feel stupid, because so many others had made the same mistakes before me. I kept working on it and learned little by little.

I really needed a website. Otherwise, no one could have found me to book me as a performing artist. Luckily, nowadays we don't really have to know a lot of programming any more to create websites. But learning the basics back then still helps me today, not only with all of my sites, but it also gave me an excellent technical understanding of a lot of things and trained my logical thinking skills. I'm actually a real techie because I always wanted to figure out how to do things on my own.

I was very fortunate to work with a very talented, experienced, and creative stage director a few years ago. She always told us singers to keep sharpening the edge of our skills, every day, perfecting our art little by little. Little things you repeatedly do can have a huge effect if you do them daily. Just imagine you had started learning a language five years ago, or had starting singing lessons a lot sooner, or started working out regularly five years ago. How much further along would you be now? What if you had done something for just 10 minutes every day for the last 5 years? How skilled would you be now?

Since we can't change the past, we can only start right here and now. But we can certainly change the future by taking action today. It's up to you what actions you do or do not take today, tomorrow, next week, next month, next year. Also, keep in mind that progress is exponential. The beginning is always the hardest and slowest since you're getting into something entirely new. You have no experience to look back on and have to start from scratch. The more skilled you become in an area, the faster you learn something new about it. Your understanding is already pretty good, so you grasp new concepts much quicker. But there will always be times when you plateau. That's especially when you need to persevere and look at everything from a different angle, maybe taking a different approach.

As a toddler, taking the first step takes the longest. The second step is a little easier, and once step ten thousand is made, it's already automatic, and the child can run, jump, and walk backward. A few years later, dancing, tapping, and gymnastics can be executed by the same legs. Considering how difficult and scary that very first step once was, it's actually amazing to have come to the point to where it is completely automatic and second nature.

So, from now on, keep working on every aspect of your skills: sing every day, and when you don't, study music, get inspired by reading artists' biographies, learn about music theory, do ear training exercises, go to concerts and hear and see what other artists do. Even doing any type of creative activity will help you as a performing artist, since you will train your brain to improvise and think outside the box. You will get so much better at improvising and doing something on the spur of the moment when you're actually performing.

Just like an actor invests countless hours into improv exercises, you should do the same. Yes, creativity can actually be trained. If you think you're not very creative and are scared of improvising, putting yourself in situations that push you beyond your comfort zone will undoubtedly help you develop as an artist.

As you get better at dealing with situations that are random and unforeseeable, you also learn to cope with stress and eventually stress less. Stress has an adverse effect on your body, especially when it becomes a constant state.

When it's an isolated event, such as when you get up on stage and get nervous, or the band does something entirely unexpected during your performance and you have to improvise to keep the show going, adrenalin suddenly shoots through your body and causes shortness of breath, a faster heart rate, shaking, shivering, and a loss of focus and concentration. When you live through situations like these, again and again, you eventually learn that there is actually no threat and your body doesn't go into fight or flight mode. You learn to stay calm and know that it's not the end of the world.

Constant stress is the kind of stress that is really bad for your body and hence also for your instrument. Constant stress makes you sick, both psychologically and physically. One of the main factors of so many diseases today is continuous stress.

Sleep deprivation, high expectations to function with little or no rest, the fast-paced world we live in, the shift from being treated like an individual to becoming a mere number in a system that doesn't respect your uniqueness, can make you sick. We are definitely not all the same, but we are often treated as such. It already begins in childhood, when every child in the class has to learn the exact same material and has to follow the same learning style. What about the fact that it is absolutely natural for every child to have different strengths? Instead of excelling in a few areas, everyone is required to be mediocre in all areas. Some are more visual learners, others need to touch and experiment, yet others learn best through listening and repeating. Not respecting your personality in what you do every day will put stress on you that could easily be avoided.

I'm just saying that this constant stress that often begins in childhood and continues throughout our lives, is not exactly contributing to a healthy body and mind.

How can we as singers escape this, while still integrating into this world? I believe there can be a balance between the things we have to do and fostering a positive attitude toward them to express ourselves in our own world of creativity. Singing can be so freeing and an awesome counterpart to that other side. It's all about avoiding the constant stress that comes with a negative attitude.

What if the demands that weigh us down - let's say the IRS, paperwork, possibly a full-time job we have to execute although we hate it - could be seen as something positive? It's all about your attitude. Since I've been diving deep into personal development, reading every book and listening to every podcast I can find to learn about improving myself and my mindset, my attitude towards many things that used to stress me out has changed a lot. I wake up every morning looking forward to what I will get to do. Even those things that I don't necessarily love doing, I see as a means to an end. They're just part of life - like sun and shade. One doesn't exist without the other. And I can actually find joy in things by adding little elements such as motivating music or using a Pomodoro method app.

And you better believe that less stress and more positivity will have an impact on your instrument as well as your performance. How could you sing freely when you feel weighed down? I don't think it's really possible to express yourself freely and to even take in an open, deep breath without first getting rid of the stress that makes you tense and narrows your perception.

You want to be able to use all of your senses to their fullest extent, not be dulled down by a haze of constant negativity and stress.

Your instrument consists of your whole being: body, mind, and spirit. You must take care of every aspect. If you do this, you have taken another step forward toward becoming the best singer you can possibly be.

LARYNX POSITION

I've heard every take on the larynx position over the years. There are a lot of different approaches out there when it comes to the position and role of the larynx in singing, also depending on the genre.

One prevalent practice, especially in classical singing, is that you must lower the larynx to achieve a desirable sound. This is especially true when it comes to opera singing, and mostly sopranos seem to be taught that way to obtain a bigger sound.

I've encountered many students in my studio who had taken lessons from other teachers before and were quite confused, to say the least. They were taught to sing with a low larynx position but still were not quite happy with their voice. In my experience, the lowered larynx is a quick fix to achieve a fuller and more voluminous as well as darker voice color. When you lower the larynx, it's almost like pushing a button to go on full boost, and it works quite well. But let me tell you why I'm not a friend of the lowered larynx: I've seen nothing but problems resulting from this technique.

The larynx does indeed lower naturally as you sing higher and higher. However, there's a distinct difference between allowing it to lower naturally and pushing it down excessively.

First of all, when you push down the larynx, you are not using enough of your head frequencies to produce more bright overtones, which are the frequencies that really carry the tone through space. Lowering the larynx may have the effect of creating a perceived louder tone. However, that's only the case when we talk about the sheer volume that's produced at the source of the sound. If we want to talk about a quality of tone that doesn't die off at arm's length, we have to put forth a lot more effort than just pushing down the larynx.

I was rehearsing a duet from Rigoletto with a tenor once, and I honestly had to hold my left ear shut, which was where he was standing, simply because he was so incredibly loud that it hurt my ears. It was insane, and I couldn't believe how much volume came out of him. However, when we performed the entire opera in the theater with the orchestra playing, his voice was drowning on the recording, while you could always hear my voice float right on top of the orchestra.

I got to see the video that was recorded during the performance, and I know that the mics were positioned in the back of the auditorium. The result really surprised me back then, especially since after some of my auditions I had been repeatedly told that my voice wasn't big enough. But even without massive volume, I was always able to sing over the orchestra, as long as I made sure I opened up the resonance so that the sound had shimmer and sparkle. This is the true art of singing. There are no quick fixes, and if there seems to be one, you should always be suspicious - it may not actually deliver results that are sustainable in the long run.

Another problem that results from a larynx that is pushed down continuously is an altered voice color that isn't natural and will at some point cause strain on your voice. By pushing the larynx down over an extended period, the air doesn't flow naturally, and the vocal tract is not in a natural phonation position. Have you ever tried to talk while yawning? Really hard, isn't it? It's because your larynx is pushed way down when you yawn. I have experimented quite a bit with larynx position, and the only approach that felt easy without any strain on my voice was the neutral larynx position.

However, when I say neutral larynx position, I mean that it is allowed to move naturally without constraints, including the natural lowering on higher pitches. It is absolutely natural for your larynx to move up and down as you form different vowels at different pitches. If you gently put your fingers on your throat right where the larynx sits, you will feel a vibration as well as a movement as you speak. The same happens when you sing. This is absolutely natural, and you want this to happen. Otherwise, you wouldn't be able to shape language.

However, pushing the larynx down with force, or raising it for that matter, will keep it from moving up and down naturally. This movement is necessary though to prevent continuous strain on your vocal cords. As you push the larynx in either a high or low position, the air stream that passes through your vocal cords is altered in intensity and direction, and muscles are not coordinated correctly, which won't allow you to sing with ease for many years to come.

In my experiments with larynx position, I have tried different positions on high belted pitches, as well as low soft pitches and high head voice. I found that using the larynx for voice color to express emotions is wonderful since it allows you to create so many different sounds and colors. However, I only ever do this for short moments, never a prolonged period. As a matter of fact, pushing the larynx down or up when I sang high belted pitches, caused a scratching sensation in my throat and I felt fatigued quite quickly after doing this.

Working with my students, I have made it a mission to make them aware of the larynx position and how it alters the sound, and so many - especially those who had voice lessons before - say that the neutral position feels so much better and helps them find more ease in singing.

Essentially, you always want to take as much work and strain as possible off of your vocal cords, and do the hard work elsewhere, such as in your support and by using the resonating spaces most efficiently to amplify the sound and create more overtones.

There are so many voice teachers who actually teach a consistently low larynx position, but physiologically, it makes no sense. I always try to find ways to achieve more ease in singing, ultimately making the techniques I use and teach sustainable, so they can be utilized to help anyone sing in a healthy way for a long time to come. I've put all kinds of different approaches to the test while singing many hours a week, combining genres from opera, oratorio and art song to jazz, pop, and rock. I had to find a way of singing that took the strain off my voice, and I can honestly say that I've never had any vocal problems.

We all know the stories of so many famous and successful singers who had to cancel tours or take breaks due to vocal problems, Adele and Bonnie Tyler only being two of them. Good technique really shows once an artist does a lot of singing all the time.

There are way too many cases of singers who used to have a beautifully resonant and clear voice but became increasingly raspy due to bad lifestyle choices and singing technique. While a raspy voice can certainly have its positive sides in regards to the sound quality (yes, tastes vary!), there are usually life long consequences. Some singers will never be able to sing a clean tone again due to irreversible damage to the vocal cords.

Master Your Voice

To name a few singers whose voice deteriorated throughout their career: Joe Cocker, Janis Joplin, and Kelly Clarkson. While these still were and are incredible artists and have great voices and skill, their way of singing clearly has caused some irreversible damage. There are many singers with less than great vocal habits that cause problems repeatedly, so don't fall into the trap of imitating the sound of your favorite singers. Their technique may not be healthy.

I know you don't want that to happen to you, and while a raspy sound can be totally cool, you should have the knowledge about how raspiness can be created and how this affects your vocal cords. I'm a big fan of "everything in moderation," not only in life but also when it comes to singing technique. You may have some raspiness or dark sound at times, but you should only do it consciously and purposefully.

VIBRATO

Wikipedia defines vibrato as a "musical effect consisting of a regular, pulsating change of pitch." But what is it good for, and how does one create it?

One thing is for sure: some just do it right from the beginning, and some don't.

Vibrato is a topic that creates many controversies. Some vocal coaches teach vibrato with a very technical approach. They show their students to alternate between two neighboring pitches and then speed it up little by little. Some even teach giving an accent to a pitch with the diaphragm and then speeding that accentuation up.

I don't believe in teaching vibrato in a very technical sense, other than getting an initial feel for it since it will most likely not create a natural, consistent and even vibrato, but rather a shaking or wobbling pitch. While exercises such as alternating between pitches can be useful to get an idea of what vibrato feels like and where it happens, I don't think they help in developing vibrato in a way that won't be overemphasized and artificial. It will most likely be too big, slow, or too wide.

Although most well-known singers have vibrato, not all of them do. The use of vibrato and its importance really depends on the genre and intensity level.

In bel canto, for instance, vibrato is desired and is present at almost any moment. The reason is obvious: it helps with a better placement of the resonance and takes some of the strain off of the vocal cords when singing pieces that put extremely high demands on them.

However, in a lot of ancient music, before baroque, the singing practice often included straight tone singing as well as tremolo instead of vibrato. So, vibrato definitely is also a stylistic tool.

Even in popular mainstream music of the last few centuries, the use of vibrato has changed. When you watch old musical movies from the 40s and 50s, pay attention to how vibrato is used. You will hear a fast, dense vibrato that's there at almost any moment. In contemporary pop music, on the other hand, its use has changed quite a bit. A lot of straight tone singing with only narrow and rather fast vibrato in particular moments. From now on, pay attention to the way an artist uses vibrato when you listen to the radio or your favorite recordings or music videos. Singing style, as well as the use of vibrato, has changed over the decades.

If you have a natural vibrato, you should train to become more aware of when and how you use it so you can utilize it better to your advantage. Not having any vibrato can be as problematic as not being able to sing without it. Ideally, you are always in control and use it exactly when you want to.

What I often notice is that those singers who naturally have vibrato use it too much. This prevents the singer from building up any tension in the music since a straight tone resolving into a vibrato gives the impression of having arrived at a resting point whenever the vibrato sets in.

Can you sing vibrato only on soft pitches, or can you add it no matter how high or low, or what dynamic level you sing? You should practice vibrato by adding or subtracting it from a tone without changing any other quality of the tone. Keep the same dynamics and tone color. If you notice that you can only add vibrato when you soften your voice, you have something to work on.

If you're someone who has natural vibrato, I suggest you practice alternating straight tones and pitches with vibrato. Begin singing a pitch straight, then add the vibrato. Or, begin with vibrato and then stop the vibrato. Then start singing a soft pitch and as you crescendo add vibrato. In reverse, start singing loudly and add the vibrato only when you get softer. Try this throughout your range, and you will notice that some of these exercises will be more difficult than others. For most beginners, it's more challenging to add vibrato on high and loud pitches. You have a way that you naturally use vibrato. But only once you become conscious about how you do it and what exactly you do, can you actually control it. Don't let it control you. A lack of control limits the possibilities of how you can use it to express music adequately.

Vibrato is also a great measuring tool for your support and placement.

A wobbly, wide vibrato usually means that there's not any consistent support and even breath flow. A very fast and narrow, almost shaky vibrato indicates too much tension and tightness. I always notice that on days when I feel tired and worn-out, my vibrato isn't as nice as it could be. It gets wider and slower, possibly uneven, which means the pitch isn't as accurate. On days when I have perfect placement in my resonance and feel like I'm well centered in my core, it gets very even and suits the music I'm singing very well because I'm in control.

Vibrato can make or break a song. Take the song "I will always love you" in the Whitney Houston version, for instance: in the chorus, Whitney sings that high pitch on "I" straight and doesn't add vibrato until a few seconds later. This signals a forward movement and tension in the music to the listener. Imagine Whitney's voice starting vibrato as soon as she begins the pitch and keeping it for the entire phrase. It would sound quite different, wouldn't it?

Vice versa, imagine the famous Puccini aria "Nessun Dorma" from Turandot without any vibrato on the high "vincero." It would sound yelled and screamed and not nice and round, no matter how beautiful the tenor's voice is.

Having sung a lot of opera, I can't imagine singing those very high soprano pitches without vibrato, as it would sound very screechy. The vibrato adds intention, warmth, and shimmer. One of my opera coaches always made this gesture with her hands, placing her pointer finger into the palm of her other hand and wiggling it lightly. She did this whenever I sang a high pitch, even when it was a very short one. Adding a little bit of vibrato on those very high tones gave it so much more brightness and a better resonance because the pitch was no longer static and tense. Vibrato adds in more frequencies since it is a slight variation.

On passages with a lot of tension between the vocal cords, vibrato helps loosen up the tenseness so that you can sing longer without getting strained.

Vibrato can be wonderful, but it can also be very distracting when it's not used correctly.

CONNECTION & DIRECTION

There's a huge difference both in the way you sing and the effect in has on your sound depending on how much you connect your phrases and give your vocal line shape and direction. I often hear singers who sing through the pitches without any kind of connection and every pitch almost seems to stand alone. It becomes very choppy and robotic. Try speaking without having a clear direction in mind, without knowing where you want to go or shaping the dynamics accordingly. There are ups and downs, tension and release, slight tempo variations, accents, heavy and light syllables. It would be so much harder to make sense out of what you say without all of these elements. They're what makes us human and helps us express our intentions and emotions. But that's precisely where a lot of singers fail. There's just no flow, no purpose, no direction in the singing. No thought is put into the flow of the melody and harmony or even the subtle articulation of the words.

You may think these are just little nuances that the average audience wouldn't even be able to perceive. But don't ever underestimate your audience! Although these seem to be very subtle nuances in expression, these are the elements that help your audience make sense of what you're singing and allow them to connect with you on a deeper level. Your audience may not be able to describe what it is, but they will feel somewhat disconnected and slightly confused in regards to the meaning of the song you're singing.

Let's talk about the positive effect connection and direction has on your singing technique. Imagine wanting to throw a baseball to a pitcher who then will hit it with a bat. You would first look at the exact spot you want the ball to be thrown, estimate the speed it needs to have, then inhale as you reach back before you propel it forward. If you didn't have a clear direction in mind, all of your body's movements wouldn't be coordinated and connected, and the ball would most likely never reach its intended destination.

The same thing happens with the sound waves your vocal cords create. They need to have a clear direction, or else they get stuck and won't move forward. When you think of a direction, it will help you open up the resonating spaces, increase the engagement of your core for support, and minimize tension in other places that would block the sound.

Have you ever noticed that when you try something really hard, your whole body gets stiff and tense, even when you don't need your whole body to be involved? Have you ever watched someone play video games and move around their entire body as if they were a contortion artist as they were navigating the character in the game? All the actually have to do is move their thumbs on the remote pad. But they seem to have a better sense of direction when they use the whole body.

When you sing, you need to have a sense of direction without actually moving your body. Having said that, a clear sense of direction will make a huge difference. You will take deeper breaths, and connect through the phrase without just aiming for that high pitch, but holding on to that support until there's an actual point of release. Music has a flow and direction, without which it would sound robotic. Shaping the subtle details within a musical phrase is only possible when you have that sense of direction.

Did you know that you can also connect through breaks and rests? If you keep your support in place through a rest, your next entrance will be so much more accurate, and you won't lose your audience's interest because you've lost tension and have given a signal of release. Keeping your focus on the direction of the musical phrase and the one that's to come will make it so much easier to convey the meaning of what you're singing.

Often times, we just focus on the hard part, work our way up to it, climax in an outburst of tension, and then let it all fall apart as soon as that difficult part is over. That's not a very efficient use of energy, as this will exhaust you over time, building up and letting go constantly. Not keeping your support when you're singing through easy passages will most likely have you singing with less than perfect technique, which will begin to strain your vocal cords.

Just think of a goalkeeper on the soccer field: his body is always alert and keeps the right kind of tension which will allow him to move quickly within a split second when necessary. If he just relaxed his body whenever there seems to be no threat and were just chilling out at the pole, it would take way too long for him to get moving once a player kicks the ball toward the goal with force. The alertness needs to be there at any moment.

So, next time you sing, make sure you stay alert by always keeping your support muscles and your posture in an ideal place that will allow you to react quickly.

I remember working with a vocal coach several years back, as I was preparing for the lead role of Gilda in Verdi's "Rigoletto." We worked on the famous aria „Caro Nome," which became one of my signature arias. For almost a full hour we worked on connecting the first phrase, which consists of short notes interspersed with rests after each note. I got so frustrated trying to connect something that mainly consisted of breaks. I tried and tried, but my coach was still not happy with the result. Now I understand what he was trying to teach me: he wanted me to keep not only the tension in my support and body but also keep the audience's attention glued to my vocal line. There were very subtle nuances in dynamics and vowel color that were definitely different once I had a true sense of connection throughout the phrase.

It's really a shame that in a lot of popular music nowadays, the shaping of a musical phrase often gets so overly simplified that the meaning is mostly lost unless you really listen to the words. I think that the meaning should still come through even if someone doesn't understand the language a song is sung in. That would be the ultimate test for an artist to prove their artistry in expressiveness. There's definitely a musical aspect to the meaning and intention of a piece of music, not only the lyrics. You would change the melodious shape of your phrases even in your speaking depending on what you're trying to express. Whenever you're exhilaratingly excited, you will definitely have a whole different level of energy than at times when you're sad and gloomy. Why is it then that in so much of popular music this aspect of the human voice is largely neglected?

Your audience wants to go on a journey with you, be emotionally involved in the song and story, sympathize with you, empathize with you. Give them what they long for!

Maybe we're already so used to hearing singers perform this way that we don't even expect anyone to be very expressive any more. Having a background in opera, I've learned how important those details are.

While I do think that the level of expressiveness and the kind of color of your voice that's expected depends on the specific genre, I still don't quite understand how anyone can sing about being heartbroken without this being reflected in their voice color and sense of direction at all. When you're devastated and sing the word "pain" for instance, I should be able to feel the pain in that word. It most certainly shouldn't sound the same as "happy" and vice versa. It's almost comical to me how some singers sing about heart-wrenching experiences, such as being dumped by the love of their life, but it actually sounds like they're not emotionally involved at all. They might as well sing about the weather forecast. It just sounds casual and unimportant. I think no matter what genre you sing in, there's always some room for expressiveness without sacrificing proper technique.

Many of my students love singing power ballads, such as the 80s classics "I will always love you" or "The Power of Love." These are not easy to sing since they have a broad range as well as long sustained high pitches that need to sound as if they're floating up there with ease, without any apparent strain. Key elements here are a really good sense of support and maintaining it throughout the song as well as an open sound that's not covered up or blocked, which means the singer needs to relax the jaw as well as use all of the resonating space in an ideal way. Always breathing freely and deeply and making sure to economize the breath throughout the long phrases is really essential.

But there's one easy principle that will make everything easier: connection and direction. When you hold that long high pitch that's the climax of the song, don't just let it sit there statically, as this will make you misplace your sound as you keep holding on to that pitch. You will get tighter and more and more tense the longer you hold that pitch until it finally will either crack because it wants to break into head voice, or it will sound narrow and shallow.

Keeping the muscles engaged that keep everything in the same placement is so much easier when you think of a forward movement. You can prevent tenseness by connecting that problematic pitch to the rest of the phrase and keeping the suspense it creates. Sometimes smoothing out the transitions from one pitch to the next can make a huge difference. So, on the long "I" in "I will always love you", don't just sit on the "I", but instead connect it to the rest of the phrase, then connect that to the next "I", shaping the ad libs on „you" in a way that anticipates what comes next. You already know the rest of the phrase and the lyrics that are about to come up, but always remember that your audience doesn't. When you shape the phrase by giving it a clear direction, your audience will also have a better sense of where you're going, when there's a stopping point and when there's forward movement.

As an exercise, try singing it in two different ways: disconnected, which only consists of very even and undifferentiated pitches without giving the phrase much shape, basically just singing pitches in sequence. Next, sing the same section in a more connected way with a sense of forward direction, anticipating the next important and emphasized word that will underline the meaning of the lyrics.

Sometimes it's the connection and direction that can give a seemingly simple song an edge and make it a lot more interesting. Some songs don't shine because of fancy ad libs, but rather because they're sung with musicality and wonderful expressiveness. Seemingly simple and easy songs can be given so much more meaning that way. That's what sets you apart from other singers: your unique way to feel and express music. Songs such as "Let it be" or "Blowin' in the Wind" may not sound spectacular, since they don't have any gigantic climaxes or dynamic ranges, but they can be given tons of life and interest by distinctively shaping the musical phrases. This is what will make someone who is listening to your cover version of these songs forget about the original and allow them to have a whole new experience with the song. You need to make it your own, giving it a meaning that is relevant to your own life.

The best compliments I ever get are when someone comes up to me and tells me this was better than the original. Or, they ask me who originally performed the song, and then they tell me that they never paid attention to the words before despite having listened to the song numerous times, but when I sang it, it made sense to them for the first time.

That's the highest praise you can get as a singer.

GOOD VS. BAD TENSION

There's a big difference between tension and strain. Without tension, you can't stand straight or keep your posture, raise your soft palate, form any open vowels, control the amount of air that passes through your vocal cords, or even close your vocal cords tightly to create high sustained pitches. Without any tension, there's no controllable sound. Just like a string on a guitar has to have a specific amount of tension to vibrate at a particular frequency, your vocals cords also do. Whenever a string on a guitar tears, it can't be played anymore, since it can't vibrate at its intended frequency anymore. And control is essential, unless you just want random noise instead of specific pitches. Our ears are accustomed to the Western music system, which consists of whole tones and semitones that have very specific frequencies.

When it comes to singing, you definitely want to have as much control over the creation of the sound as possible. While this is precisely what's so hard in the beginning, it's also the coolest achievement to have a sense of control once you get the hang of it.

I have so much fun nowadays just playing around with different sounds I can create with my voice. I can imitate just about any human sound, just because I have excellent control and know how to push all the buttons. That's only possible with the tension in exactly the right spots and lots of coordination. The RIGHT spots - that's critical. You want to create tension in those areas where you need it and minimize it in those spots where it would hinder an ideal sound.

An example of bad tension would be a tense jaw. This creates

Freya Casey

strain, which makes you compensate in other places, such as pulling back the tongue or widening your mouth horizontally. Having a relaxed jaw will also help open up the resonating spaces, as it will help you relax the back of your tongue, your cheeks, and your neck. A relaxed jaw and neck created a more rounded sound.

An interesting phenomenon about tension is that it doesn't only affect the area where it occurs. Have you ever worked out too hard and were sore the next day? Let's say, you pushed your calves too hard. The next day, you will probably alter the way you walk, trying to compensate for the painful movement your calf muscles cause. You may limp or walk crooked, which may cause your hips to hurt after a while. Once I tore a ligament in my ankle, and I couldn't use that foot for a while. However, I put a lot more weight on the other leg, and I remember that the other leg got very sore. Not only the leg but especially the knee. Any time you put too much weight on one body part, your body will try to compensate to alleviate the strain caused by bad tension.

In singing, there needs to be tension in the muscles controlling the vocal folds, i.e., the cricothyroid and arytenoid muscles. Good vocal cord closure can only happen when there's tension. There also needs to be tension to keep your soft palate lifted and your tongue in the right shape to form the vowels and consonants. When a singer gets „tongue lazy", the sound becomes nasal and less intelligible. Also in the support mechanism, without tension, the required density for high and loud pitches can't be created so that the vocal folds won't vibrate.

So, areas of good tension are vocal folds, support, soft palate and the exact right areas of the tongue and pharynx.

Areas that interfere with resonance when there's too much

tension are the neck, jaw, shoulders, the wrong areas of the tongue and pharynx and larynx.

The tricky part about coordinating the right kind of tension and relaxation is that our bodies are not used to de-coupling certain body parts from others. When you sing a high and loud tone, your tendency will always be to create more tension in your whole body as well, including your shoulders, neck, and jaw. Working hard from your support while relaxing your shoulders, neck, and jaw takes a lot of practice, but once achieved, singing can feel like floating along.

So, whenever you feel uncomfortable tension, ask yourself if it's in an area that's necessary for singing or in an area where it hinders you to sing with control and excellent resonance.

There are exercises to help you control different parts of your body separately. For example, you can stand with your back against a wall while singing fast ad-libs. Put a book on top of your head and try to balance it by keeping as still as possible. Make sure you relax your neck and sing through the phrase with the fast ad-libs. You will know if you're moving your head along too much, which means you are creating tension in your neck.

You can also stand in front of a mirror and sing a legato scale or arpeggio on a single vowel. Your jaw should not move as you move from one pitch to the next. If it keeps moving, you can use your hand to hold your jaw and gently press your cheeks in.

Be creative in your exercises to address your exact problems with bad tension that causes strain.

HOW TO CONNECT TO A SONG

Every singer has had this happen: you have just learned and memorized a song, are totally excited about performing it, because you're absolutely in love with it - but as soon as you get onto the stage or in front of your teacher and begin to sing, you don't quite feel it. You don't exactly feel the strong connection you felt when you practiced on your own. You know you didn't do the song justice and could have done so much better. It feels like you have failed.

I can tell you from my own experience: when you achieve a deep connection to the song to where you live through it as if you had just made it up on the fly, your voice begins doing things that are almost out of this world. Once you feel the true essence of a song, what it's really about, and what it means to you, a whole new world of singing opens up. Despair, deep love, urgency: once you can really connect to these feelings that in the music, your body does a lot of the right things automatically: better support, more connection, better phrasing, open throat, more accurate and expressive enunciation, more dynamics and voices colors.

A lot of these things usually take care of themselves once you are truly connected to the lyrics. In my own teaching experience, I've seen it countless times. Once the student connected to the music and lyrics on a deeper level, the accents came at the exact right time, the breath was at the right time and intensity, and the voice color was beautiful. There's something deep inside of us that intuitively knows how to communicate feelings once we are convinced we really feel them.

Here's the method I recommend if you want to get into the

habit of connecting to your songs:

The first step should be actually to read through the lyrics. You can do this before or after studying the melody, or better yet - both before and after, and in between. Each time you speak through the lyrics, they may take on a slightly different meaning as your understanding of the music evolves. Even after knowing a song for some time, it's incredible how much more there's to discover each and every time you work through it. There may be aspects you've never thought of before that are suddenly jumping out at you, just because you have recently had an experience that helps you relate to it so much better. As your life circumstances change, the way you interpret a song will also change. It's like going on an adventure each and every time you pull out a new or old song.

Read the song like a poem, but make sure you don't speak it like you're reading the sheet music. You want to sound as authentic and real as possible, making sure you use the whole range of your speaking voice and use your breath in a way that is very natural. If there's intensity in the words, it should also be in your breath. You should pay attention to speaking slowly and drawing out the vowels, while at the same time being very accurate in your enunciation of the consonants. Paint the picture with your voice and with the language. For instance, the word "crap" should sound harsh and annoyed, while the word "soothe" should sound calming and comforting. The consonants in "soothe" are soft but still very strong. The consonants in "crap" are hard and explosive, expressing precisely the meaning of the word itself. Also, make sure you make dynamic changes to convey the flow of the story. Get louder when you get excited, get soft when you are more hesitant. Give every word a motivation and a reason to exist, as if you had just created it.

Adjust the tempo slightly, pushing ahead a little when you're excited, and slowing down when you are helpless and sad. Whispering, vocal fry, raspiness, screaming, yelling, sobbing... go as far as you possibly can, while keeping in mind the principles for good breathing and support and utilizing the different voice colors in a healthy way. Once you have explored all of these possibilities and actually used all of these different sounds to express yourself vocally, you will have a much more concrete idea of what you're singing about in the song.

The next step I think can help so much in connecting to a song, is taking one line at a time and paraphrasing it, adding the subtext it may contain.

For instance, the phrase "You're giving me a million reasons to let you go" from Lady Gaga's „Million Reasons" could be paraphrased as "I actually have so many reasons to leave you right now." The subtext could be: "I could totally leave you in an instance. I have tons of reasons, and everybody would understand why I have to do it. That time when you just treated me like a stranger when I came to your office... that really hurt me. And when I expressed my feelings, you acted like I was the one doing everything wrong. You never took my feelings seriously, and this hurt me so much."

Speaking out the subtext in your own language, in your own words, will help you connect to the song, so it becomes a part of you. Find some subtext that refers to some situation in your life that has really happened. Remembering what really happened will make it even more real to you, and you will connect to your emotions.

Now it's time to connect with the music. Pay attention to

when the melody line rises, and how the harmonies move along. Is there a dissonance? Does it finally resolve? Is there a smooth connection or are there short staccato pitches that are disconnected? Most good composers have something specific in mind when they compose, and they do it with intention, so it's your job to take the cues that are in the music or the arrangement and interpret their meaning and significance.

The reason for that high belted out note may be that you're supposed to be genuinely ecstatic and put all of your energy into announcing to the world what you can't no longer contain.

If there's a loud moment followed by a sudden rest and a moment of silence, the reason for that may be that you just realized how unspeakable what you're feeling is, so you suddenly hold your breath for a moment as you are beginning to grasp reality. There's so much meaning packed into music. You just have to find it.

If you want to see this principle in action, you can pay attention to the music in a great movie. Without the music, there would be no logical motivation for a lot of the actors' actions. But more than their actions, the feelings are masterfully illustrated and emphasized by the music. Imagine "ET" without the music, or "Titanic," or "Mission Impossible," or "James Bond." The actors would only be half as powerful without the music. Try watching any horror movie without the music - it will almost seem like a comedy and look very silly. The music usually precedes the actions or emotions that are intended to be evoked.

When you sing, you want to create the illusion that you're the one creating the sounds on the spot. Everything needs to have a motivation that comes from inside of you, even when there's a guitar solo or an instrumental interlude, an intro or outro. Make the music happen as if it only happens because you're thinking and feeling it.

Once you truly connect to the song, you will not only enjoy performing it so much more, but you will also be so much more authentic and will touch your audience on a much deeper level. The fun really only comes once you dive deep into the meaning of a song. Every high pitch begins to make sense, and there's a flow to it that would never be there if you hadn't done the work of diving deeper into the lyrics and music and looking for the meaning.

The remarkable thing about all of this is, that as you keep training that muscle of connecting to a song, it becomes easier and easier. After doing this for many years, I can say that I have achieved a high degree of mastery in the art of finding something I can connect with and immediately making it my own. I can open up a songbook and begin to play a song that I've never heard or sung before, and I automatically pull out all of the emotions and associations that help me connect to the music and lyrics. I can make sense of what is happening in the music almost immediately. This took lots of intentional practice.

Much of this has been trained in years of improvisation exercises and just learning new repertoire times and times again, including singing lead roles in operas. Another way that will significantly help you connect to a song and memorize the lyrics is actually acting out the song and staging it. Translating every phrase into motion and linking it to an action, a gesture, or a facial expression, or a prop, will help you engrave it into your memory so much more deeply and creates memory triggers.

You have probably heard of people who have memorized phone books or really long numbers and done so relatively quickly. They don't have a brain that works better or faster, they simply have trained their memory to connect abstract pieces of information such as numbers or words to concrete pictures in their mind. They have trained to see patterns and compartmentalize information. In music, there are definitely patterns that keep recurring. This helps to grasp patterns in ad-libs, melodies, or harmonic progression.

I've never really trained my memory other than in the area of music, but I've read a lot about the strategies for memorizing. For instance, instead of memorizing the abstract number sequence 3-5-1-6-5-9-3-0, which has no meaning in and of itself, you can imagine the following situation: 1. You're invited to your friend's 35th birthday party (3 -5). 2. As you approach the doorstep, there's 1 doorbell (1). 3. You ring the doorbell 6 times, as many pitches as the first line of „Happy Birthday to You" has. You sing along with the doorbell (6). 4. When your friend opens the door, you high-five each other (5). 5. There's a birthday cake with 9 skittles on top because your friend love to play skittles as a hobby (9). 6. His wife and little daughter are also there, which means you celebrate the birthday with 3 other people (3). 7. You signal to your friend that the cake is delicious with your hand shaping an „o" with your fingers (0).

Do you see how you can memorize things by replacing abstract information with a more meaningful image?

You can do the same with lyrics: acting out the song will help you create concrete pictures in your mind and connect triggers to cues in the music. This enables you to remember the images you have created in your mind and the words that are connected to them. Acting out also makes it so much easier to figure out which hand gestures are natural and appropriate. There's nothing worse than a singer who constantly stays locked in a typical singer's pose such as extending one arm in front of the body or even folding their hands in front of their chest. This is very distracting to someone who's watching since it looks very premeditated and inauthentic. No one would ever talk and tell a story that way.

Hand gestures should always happen where they naturally would: usually around the mid-torso area since you typically want the person you're talking to see your gestures. You wouldn't gesture way down beside your hips. But this is precisely what happens when you're insecure in front of others when you sing and don't follow through with the gestures. When you do the gestures only halfway, and hesitantly, that will undoubtedly look awkward and unnatural.

Pay attention to how you gesture while you talk to someone, especially when you are having a conversation about something that is very important to you. Urgency increases the intensity in your hand and facial gestures. Your energy should be reflected in your gestures and expressions.

Another wonderful side-effect of getting into a routine of practicing connection with your songs is that your voice will automatically do things that would be very difficult to explain on a purely technical level. Explaining exactly when it makes sense to use vocal fry, breathiness, glottal attack, a narrow throat, lighter or heavier tones, would be a crazy undertaking. It's important to learn these principles. Whenever you're truly connected to a song that expresses despair, there are be moments of vocal fry onset that make sense. When you are screaming out of anger, it's only logical that you should use a heavy chest voice instead of a light, breathy sound. Your intention determines the sound of your voice.

See how essential it is to connect to your songs? You have to do it to communicate the meaning. Otherwise, no one will believe you and their mind will wander off during your performance wondering what's for dinner tonight.

Connect to enjoy the song, and enjoy to connect!

RESONANCE

What makes your voice sound like you?

There's no question about it: you would always recognize the voice of your mom, husband, friend, children, or any other person you have known for a while unless they have a bad cold. Everyone's voice is unique, although there may be similarities and some people even straight up sound the same. The voice is very much part of everyone's identity and personality, just like the way you look. But even twins or lookalikes do have distinctive differences. The voice is just as unique as everything else about a human being.

Have you ever watched a foreign movie with voice-overs? You don't hear the voices of the actors you see on the screen, and when you observe carefully, you can see that the words the actor shapes with the mouth are not what you hear. Having grown up in Germany, I have grown accustomed to movies with voice-over artists who speak the voices for actors like Bruce Willis, Arnold Schwarzenegger, Whoopi Goldberg, Sean Connery and many more. For most Germans, Arnold Schwarzenegger's voice is the one of his voice-over artist. No Austrian accent. German without dialect. Occasionally, a different actor fills in to synchronize the voice, which throws most people off and they don't like it. It's like someone has given the actor a different identity, and it can be annoying. Imagine looking at someone you know, and suddenly they speak with a different voice. That would not only be strange, but the voice also wouldn't seem to suit that person, since the voice is very much part of someone's identity and personality.

But what is it that makes a voice so distinguishably unique?

Master Your Voice

First of all, there are factors like vocal cord anatomy, how large, how long, how thick, how symmetric they are. Another factor that shapes the sound of the voice is bone structure and the shape and position of all other parts involved in vocalization: larynx, pharynx, cricothyroid, arytenoid, tongue, epiglottis, and many more. These are all genetically predetermined, and you're just born with a specific set of vocal prerequisites.

However, since a lot of those parts involved in phonation are not static, the sound of the voice can be influenced, which makes a considerable difference in singing. Directing the sound waves intentionally affects resonance, which is what we continuously try to tweak through our singing lives to sing more effectively.

Picture an old gramophone, the kind that you have to wind up mechanically with a hand crank so that the turntable rotates. It also has a big sound horn to amplify and project the sound created by the needle gliding across the surface of the record. When you put your ear right next to the needle while the record is rotating, you can actually hear the music very softly. The sound is amplified simply by the large resonating body of the sound horn. A large empty space amplifies sound because it reflects the sound waves. The same applies to a piano. There are different sizes of pianos: shorter ones and taller ones. While the strings are pretty much the same, the quality of the wood and the size of the body around the strings can vary quite a lot. A piano with a smaller body will not nearly sound as full and loud as one with a larger resonating space. A grand piano sounds huge enormous in comparison to a small piano. The sound waves have a place to be reflected and to make what surrounds them vibrate, in this case, the wooden body.

It's the same principle with guitars. An electric guitar does not have a resonating body, so the sound waves that are created by the vibration of the strings don't get amplified. You can hear sound coming from the strings, but only very softly. The electric guitar needs to be electrically amplified, while an acoustic guitar has its own resonating body to amplify the sound waves.

When it comes to the voice, you can either direct the sound waves into the resonating body surrounding them or close off the pathways that allow the sound to disperse throughout your head and cause different structures to vibrate along. That's why lifting the soft palate, for instance, is so important. When you raise it, the sound waves can move into the mouth, which is a pretty big space for resonance. When you leave that pathway very narrow, the sound can only move toward your nose, which is a much smaller resonating space.

You can easily hear the difference by beginning to sing an open and loud „ah" and then putting your hand over your open mouth. Don't shut it off completely, but you will notice how drastically the sound changes as you slowly close up the opening. Your hand stops the sound waves from traveling any further, so a lot less sound makes it to your ears.

I think it's so cool that you can influence the sound of your voice so much. You can make it sound darker, brighter, fuller, smaller, brassy, pingy, or breathy, depending on the desired sound at any given moment in a song. The different places of resonance in your body can be combined in endless ways, allowing for a plethora of voice colors. The larynx, the soft palate, the pharynx, the chest, the tracheal tree, the oral and the nasal cavity are all resonators that can amplify, intensify, enrich, improve, and filter the sound of your voice.

When you sing in chest voice, there's more resonance in the

chest area than in the head. You can easily feel the vibrations when you put your hand on your chest while you sing or speak in lower to mid-chest voice. As you raise the pitch, there's more and more resonance in your head. In fact, you can picture the resonance going upward from your chest and mouth area, and as the pitch gets higher, the vibration also happens higher and higher in your head, all the way to the forehead. The fascinating thing is that you can still influence how much of any of these areas resonates when you sing a given pitch. That's why the mixed register is so hard to grasp, although it's mainly a mix of resonance. You can be in a mix of resonances, both while being in the heavy mechanism as well as in the head mechanism. You can sing higher chest voice pitches with either more chest resonance or more head resonance. The same is true for pitches that are sung in head voice which aren't very high yet.

Let's get into some more detail about how to achieve better resonance. First and foremost, be aware of your jaw and its position, especially if there's any tension. You can check if your jaw is relaxed by slightly opening your mouth and moving your head back and forth. Your mouth should open as you tilt your head backward and close as you tilt your head forward. Only when you relax the jaw, will you be able to shape an open and round resonating space in your mouth and throat, which together create a large area of resonance. Opening the jaw extremely wide usually causes the tongue to be pulled back and block the way. Not opening the mouth enough will make it too narrow to create a substantial resonating space. The jaw position is something you can easily check by looking at yourself in a mirror while you sing or record yourself on video. You should make sure that the opening of the jaw is almost the same, whether you sing high or low. Resist the urge to open too much when you sing high or closing too much when you sing low. Especially on the low end of your voice, you need to create a nice resonating space to achieve a warm and beautiful tone, since the vocal cords can't usually generate a lot of volume any more as you relax into those low pitches.

Once your jaw is relaxed, you also need to make sure you relax the tongue. Further back in your throat is where most of the action takes place. The area behind the uvula is called the pharynx. Most people would just call it the throat. Sing an "ah" vowel, beginning on a higher pitch and then moving down the scale. To keep the vowel the same, you will have to change the position of your soft palate and tongue slightly. Otherwise, the "ah" becomes an „uh" or "eh." You will feel that the sound of the vowel changes a lot as you change the shape of your tongue and pharynx.

Did you know that every vowel has its own overtone frequencies in addition to the pure pitch that is created by the vibration of your vocal cords? That's why for some pitches, a slight alteration of the vowel can totally change their resonance and make them feel easier or harder to sing.

When you sing, you shape the vowels very similarly to the way you do when you speak, but you have to think everything a little bit bigger and longer in duration. Since you want your audience to understand the lyrics, make sure you shape vowels and consonants correctly, depending on the language you sing in. An "ee" isn't as narrow as you most people think. The tongue only lifts between your back teeth, but the soft palate is lifted while the tip of the tongue is relaxed. Go from an "ah" (as in „far") to an "eh" (as in „bed"), then to an "ee" (as in „me") without moving your jaw much, just keeping it relaxed. Focus only on moving your tongue, soft palate, and pharynx. You will notice that there are very specific parts that move, but it isn't always your whole mouth with lots of jaw movement. At the same time, always keep your cheeks relaxed and don't pull them sideways when you sing "eh" or "ee", as this will make the resonating space very narrow and eliminate valuable overtones that can't vibrate when you don't have an open and round space for resonance.

Starting at the front of your mouth, there's the tip of the tongue, the tongue body, and the tongue root. The pharynx is the space behind your tongue and the area that can be seen when you yawn with your mouth wide open. You can also see the uvula, which is attached to the soft palate. Further back is the epiglottis, which closes off the trachea. When you hold your breath underwater and close the epiglottis, there won't be any air flowing through your trachea, which means you can't inhale or exhale through your nose or mouth. Even having your mouth open will not allow any air to flow as long as the epiglottis is closed. Also, when you swallow, the epiglottis automatically closes, so that no food or drink can go down the wrong pipe.

Further down are the vocal cords, which also means that no food or drink can ever touch the vocal cords since the epiglottis won't allow anything to get into the trachea under normal circumstances. If that were the case, your body would instantly react by coughing to propel any foreign object out of the trachea.

The soothing sensation of drinking warm tea or taking throat lozenges comes from soothing the area that lies above the epiglottis. When you have a cold, the pharynx is usually affected by the infection, which can make swallowing and singing painful, since you have to move the whole area in your throat. Swallowing hurts because part of the mucosa in your throat get destroyed and are inflamed. Drinking warm tea alleviates the pain because it re-moisturizes reduces the swelling.

The vocal cords are surrounded by the false vocal cords (vestibular fold), cartilage tissue, and different muscles that control the vocal cords. There are several muscles involved. You don't have to know all of them, but here's a list them:

Intrinsic

Cricothyroid muscle lengthens and tense the vocal folds.

Posterior cricoarytenoid muscles abduct and externally rotate the arytenoid cartilages, resulting in abducted vocal folds.

Lateral cricoarytenoid muscles adduct and internally rotate the arytenoid cartilages, increase medial compression.

Transverse arytenoid muscles adduct the arytenoid cartilages, resulting in adducted vocal folds.

Oblique arytenoid muscles narrow the laryngeal inlet by constricting the distance between the arytenoid cartilages.

Thyroarytenoid muscles: sphincter of the vestibule, narrowing the laryngeal inlet, shortening the vocal folds, and lowering voice pitch. The **internal thyroarytenoid** is the portion of the thyroarytenoid that vibrates to produce sound.

Extrinsic

Sternothyroid muscles depress the larynx.

Omohyoid muscles depress the larynx.

Sternohyoid muscles depress the larynx.

Thyrohyoid muscles elevate the larynx.

Digastric muscle elevates the larynx.

Stylohyoid muscle elevates the larynx.

Mylohyoid muscle elevates the larynx.

Geniohyoid muscle elevates the larynx.

Hyoglossus muscle elevates the larynx.

Genioglossus muscle elevates the larynx.

As you can imagine, there are so many ways to shape and move the tongue, pharynx, soft palate, and larynx and coordinate with all of the muscles involved in phonation and resonance. Right below the vocal cords is the larynx. The area directly surrounding your larynx and vocal cords is called the voice box, since this is where the sound is created. This process is called phonation.

Just in the process of phonation, there can already be considerable differences in sound depending on the air pressure that predominates the stream of air passing through the vocal folds. Another factor is vocal cord closure. While very tight closure will create a tone that's more clear, a loose vocal cord closure will result in a breathy sound, in which you hear other frequencies, like those of the air passing through the vocal folds without being transformed into a vocal fold vibration. There will be a hissing sound, creating friction and potentially strain instead of the desired vibration of the pitch.

The larynx position also plays a vital role in the quality of your tone. As we have already established, the larynx should be relaxed and move freely, just the way it does when you speak. Pushing down the larynx will have a quick effect on the perceived volume of your voice and will seemingly create a lot of great overtones that make your voice sound bigger and more brilliant. But that is not a healthy way to create the best resonance, as it does not actually generate more resonance with frequencies that carry. If you produce a full sound by putting more strain on your vocal folds and larynx while closing up the pharynx and keeping a low soft palate, the sound waves can't travel into all of the spaces that help create more resonance. This will only create vocal fatigue and if continued for long periods, permanent damage.

Your support muscles control the amount and pressure of the air that passes through your vocal cords. I actually like the Italian term used for support much better. "Apoggio" actually means "leaning." Having a balance between the density of the air column that is created by good and steady support in combination with the exact amount of vocal fold closure for a particular pitch with a specific quality of sound will help you avoid strain and sing more efficiently.

After the sound is created by the vibration of your vocal folds moving closer together with the air that passes through them, the sound waves begin moving through your head. The direction is determined by the shape that surrounds the sound waves. The most brilliant and open sound can be achieved by maximizing space. This can be accomplished by opening the throat, lifting the soft palate, and moving the tongue in a way that it doesn't block the sound from moving higher into your head, including nasal passages and sinuses.

So, from now on, begin experimenting more with all of the different positions of all the parts involved. It's actually fun to experience how the sound of your voice changes when you shape the areas of resonance differently.

PITCH CONTROL

Pitch control is at the heart of your skill as a singer. It's the foundation of our Western music and most other music all around the world since our music it consists of specific pitches. Without good pitch control, everything else you do with your voice has absolutely no positive effect. You could have the most beautiful timbre, but if you sing the wrong pitches, it will sound wrong and not at all pleasing to the ear.

Have you ever listened to a beginner violin student? Isn't it so much worse than a beginner piano student? The cause for this lies in the different nature of the instruments since the piano has predetermined pitches that can't be altered by the player, but the violin leaves it up to the player to find any given pitch, which is a lot harder to do. On a piano, a C will always be a C, and if you play the next white key above it, it can only be a D. There's nothing in between and no sliding. On the violin, on the other hand, there's no way to know where the C is, other than from experience. The student could play any frequency that lies between a C and a D.

The problem with this is, that in our Western music system, we're accustomed to having only certain frequencies as pitches, a scale's pitches always consisting of whole tone and semitone steps between them. There's no smaller subdivision than that, and if - instead of a C or C sharp a quarter tone between these two is played or sung, it doesn't sound right to our ears.

Training pitch accuracy as a singer is one of the most important things you can and should do. Even if you do have good pitch control, there will always be moments when you may be slightly off. That's why a lot of practice makes you so much stronger and accurate. More experience means better pitch control.

But how do you get better pitch control? First of all, it's important to know that there are three steps to this process: 1. Hearing what is happening in the music, for example, the piano accompaniment or the band, and understanding the pitches that you have to sing in relation to that. 2. Imagining the pitch you want to sing and knowing what it will feel like. 3. Actually producing the correct pitch.

1. When you hear music, can you identify the relationship between pitches, i.e., their direction and how far they're apart? Can you hear when they move up or down, which instrument is higher or lower? Can you hear the underlying harmony that the pitch you're about to sing needs to fit into? To train this part of the equation, it's useful to do some ear training exercises and to memorize the sounds that repeat again and again in our Western music system. Everything is built on scales and harmonies. Learn to identify intervals, different scales, major and minor harmonies, augmented and diminished chords. You will be so much more secure in regards to what pitches fit what's going on in the music.

2. This is actually the part that presents the most significant problem to a lot of singers who are not very experienced. They may hear and identify the pitch they need to sing, but don't have the experience to know how actually to sing that pitch. High pitches are often sung without enough support, and low pitches are sung with too much force or too much breathiness. Singing the exact right pitch can be learned with lots of singing and experience.

Since an instrument accompanying the singer has a much different timbre than a human voice, it's sometimes a lot harder to sing along with an instrument than with another human voice. That's why it's often easier to sing along with a recording of another singer, or better yet, of yourself. You can hear the sound quality the singer creates on every pitch, which makes it easier to match. I highly recommend practicing without singing along with another voice, because you should train yourself to sing without following another singer. You can use karaoke tracks, or even better, an accompaniment track someone made for you that is in the exact right key for your voice.

3. Even if you have the first two parts mastered, you may still fail to have excellent pitch accuracy. Actually creating the sound is often the hard part. If you have to sing a very high pitch in chest voice, you may crack on the top if you don't have proper support, don't open your throat or raise the soft palate, or if push the larynx down too much.

After carefully listening to what's happening in the music, it's absolutely essential to imagine what it will feel like in your body to sing the phrase you're about to begin, and then prepare accordingly. Like throwing a baseball, you have to prepare before the ball can fly off, depending on how far you want to ball to go. You have to prepare your body to be able to sing the upcoming phrase by inhaling enough air, having the correct amount of vocal cord closure, the right voice color, and having everything in place you need to accurately sing the phrase, just as we've discussed in the previous chapter.

Try this exercise: imagine you're going to whisper very softly to a little child to calm and soothe it, so it will eventually fall asleep. Notice what happens in your body just before you begin to whisper, how you slowly fill your lungs with just a little bit of air, just enough for a few words. Your support muscles gently tighten just a little as you're about to use your soft voice.

Master Your Voice

Now, imagine a different scenario: you're at a big shopping mall and just discovered that a fire broke out and apparently you're the first one to notice. Feel the panic and prepare to shout out "fire" so that everyone can hear you and be warned. It's a matter of life and death. Feel how your body gets stiffer, your support muscles tighten up a lot more, and how much air you're inhaling this time in preparation.

Can you tell the difference? There's an entirely different feeling in the body, even before you ever create a sound.

The more experienced you become as a singer, the better you will be at anticipating how much effort it takes to begin any given pitch or phrase.

But besides imagining the feeling in your body as you get ready to sing, you also need to imagine the sound of your own voice. I can tell you from experience that just the mere thought of a particular sound helps a lot in shaping the actual sound that comes out a few seconds later. I always notice that after listening to certain singers I love, I have the tendency to sound a lot more like them, just because I still have the sound of their voices stuck in my head. That's why it is always helpful to listen to great singers who have proper technique because you will mostly unconsciously imitate some of their good singing behaviors.

At the same time, if you listen to singers with bad singing habits, you will probably emulate those, too.

There have been studies that prove that our brains can't distinguish between the thought of doing something and actually doing it. In an experiment with beginner basketball players. One group practiced shooting hoops every day, another group just thought through the process of shooting hoops, and the third group neither thought about it nor did it.

The group that physically shot hoops, improved by 76 percent. But here's the crazy thing: the group that only shot hoops mentally, improved by 74 percent. The control group that didn't do any practicing didn't show any improvement. So, as a singer, practicing should definitely also consist of mental work and thinking through songs and passages.

Recording yourself and getting to know the sound of your voice is an integral part of achieving better pitch control. It's hard to know if you sing with accuracy while you actually sing. Your ears are in your own head, so your voice sounds different to you than to someone who's listening from the outside. I have been in many recording studio sessions singing difficult songs, and I either thought I was totally accurate in my pitch or it was hard to hear because I was singing so loudly with so much effort.

It's hard to stay objective while you're in the heat of the battle and inside of your own body. When the producer called me out on a pitch that wasn't accurate, I could have sworn that it was. But sure enough, when he played it back to me, I cringed as I the sharp pitch stick out like a sore thumb. Always record yourself to check your work and accuracy.

Be strict with yourself, very strict!

I think, pitch control is at the heart of anything you do as a singer. When the pitches are not accurate, everything you do - as great and artistic as it may be - doesn't matter. Your audience will cringe and feel like cringing when you're very obviously sharp or flat. They may not be able to name what exactly went wrong, but even the most untrained ear can hear if pitches fit together or are slightly off. Someone who says of themselves that they don't have a musical ear, may not be able to describe if something was sharp or flat, and if the timing was early or late, but almost everyone has a feeling for music being right or something being off. Don't underestimate your audience.

You also need to learn to love the sound of your voice. If you already hate the sound of your voice before you hit that high pitch, there's hardly a good chance that you will be able to make it sound great. It's like a self-fulfilling prophecy. Expecting a horrible sound and already feeling uncomfortable and embarrassed before you even sing, will only result in very inaccurate singing and a lack of support and tension. If you cringe before the pitch comes out, your breath will most likely not be sufficient, you will be tense and cause a chain of problems.

Half of the skill as a singer consists of developing the confidence to believe in your own greatness, while at the same time knowing where you must put in the work to improve. The work needs to be put in daily, behind the scenes. Once it's showtime, it's time to shine and love what you do and to trust in your instincts. Practice often and be very strict about your pitch accuracy.

Practice with an instrument or a tuning app to learn the nuances of pitch control. You will discover that some pitches of the scale feel like they're closer together than others, even though in theory they're all just a semi-tone apart. String players learn this early on. Although our Western music system is based on the well-tempered piano of J.S. Bach, which bases everything on a scale that is made up of 12 semi-tones that have an equal distance, this isn't really the case on an acoustic level. The leading tone must always be a little higher and closer to the root than, for instance, the major third from the fourth.

It's always easier to match a pitch created by another human voice since its timbre (sound quality) sounds very similar to yours. A piano sounds quite a bit different. I experience this with my students all the time. When I sing along, it's easy for them to follow along, but as soon as I play that same melody line with the piano without singing along, it's so much harder. Practice matching your own voice by recording yourself and singing along or harmonizing. You could also sing along with another singer, then with different instruments, and lastly, without anything singing or playing your melody line. It may get harder for you, depending on your experience in singing as a soloist.

Singing with karaoke tracks can be a lot of fun and useful to learn and memorize a song. But I think, the best discipline for a singer is singing in a very bare and naked environment when it comes to sound, with just a sparse accompaniment. That way, you will be able to hear all the nuances of your voice so much better, and all the impurities and inaccuracies will be so much more apparent. It's just great practice. That's why I love to hear artists doing an unplugged version of their songs. No flaws can be hidden since the voice is absolutely exposed and in the center. I recommend not singing a whole song acapella on your own until you're more experienced and can stay on key without deviating.

Singing with a microphone will be a challenge at first, but will also help you develop your ear further. It's a good idea to begin practicing with a mic early on so that by the time you will be on stage and sing through a mic, you're used to the sound. What often happens times to singers who are not experienced in singing with a mic and hearing themselves through stage monitors, is that they alter their singing technique to compensate for the louder sound. They think they have to sing more softly and don't dare to actually sing out as they would usually do. They adjust their voice instead of changing the mic position.

I have noticed that every time I sing with a PA system in a different location, the sound is different each and every time. I have to get used to the sound before really getting into the flow and feeling comfortable with the way I hear my voice. For instance, every church sounds different, even though I use the same PA and the same settings. It takes some getting used to the sound each and every time, and I usually have to tweak the settings on my mixer slightly to get the best sound for a specific space.

Standing in a corner while you sing is another excellent way to hear your voice better and a little bit more amplified. Since the sound waves bounce off the wall and come right back to your ears, this has an amplifying effect without actually putting a reverb or other effect on the vocals. I sometimes ask my students to take a songbook, open it up and hold it up in front of their face while they sing. This usually helps them hear their voices so much better and will improve their pitch accuracy.

Another way to train your hearing and pitch matching skills is to sing with headphones. I always put one side over my ear, while sliding the other one slightly off my ear so I can hear part of the sound through the headphones and part of it "dry." This is useful in preparation for any studio work you may be getting ready for. It's great to be well prepared for any kind of acoustic situation you may encounter. And believe me, there will always be surprises!

Once you feel comfortable and have mastered good pitch accuracy, singing in all kinds of different settings and scenarios will tremendously help you train your ear and accuracy to where you will hardly ever be thrown off anymore because you have so much experience. You always can just sing by knowing what it feels like to sing a specific pitch in a particular voice color.

WHAT WILL YOUR STORY BE?

When you want to build the perfect house, you need a blueprint, a strategy, the right material, a plan, the right tools, and the knowledge about all of the steps you need to take to build that house piece by piece, brick by brick, wall by wall. You first create a foundation on solid ground which the house can stand on. When you want to build the perfect voice, you also need a blueprint, a strategy, the right material, a plan, the right tools, and the knowledge how to put all the right pieces together in the correct order.

Building a firm foundation before building complex structures on top of it is essential, since otherwise they may crumble and fall. It's up to you what kind of house you build. Do you want to create one that you can build quickly but that will be blown away by the first wind gust? Or, do you want to build a house that stands firm and stands the test of time? You need to have a vision to stay motivated, and you're the one who makes the decisions that will shape your life's story.

What will your story be? No matter what you dream, you will be the one writing your own story every day. With everything you do, every exercise you tackle, every coaching session you take, every small performance in front of people you expose your voice to, with every song you pick, with every melody you rehearse, every bit and piece of music theory you understand, every opportunity you get to gig, or work with other musicians, you will add a little piece to the puzzle that finally will make up the picture that makes your story.

Will it be a story of giving up, of regrets, of getting frustrated and giving up, of shattered hopes? Or will it be a story of persistence, getting up after failure, of grit and going against the odds, following your dreams no matter what?

I know how hard it can be to believe in yourself when what your desire seems to be out of the norm. No one around you may believe that you have what it takes to be a great singer. But as long as you let what people say and think dictate what you can or cannot do, you still haven't learned a valuable lesson. It's your voice, your body, your life, your dreams. You're the only one who decides how far you can go. Are you going to listen to someone who themselves have never reached for the stars and are stuck in their lives? Or, are you going to rewrite your own story so it will be a story of success?

It will not be easy. It will be a long journey. In fact, the journey will never end as long as you live. But if you keep your eyes on the prize, you can leave a legacy. The prize is a life that's more fulfilled because you didn't give up and kept pursuing what you love. No regrets, because you just went on and on to see how much further you can go. When you think you're at your limit, just take one more step.

Follow and learn from people who've gone before you and who have achieved what you want to achieve. Learn from the best and make sure you become better each and every day. Don't compare yourself to others, but to yourself. There's a reason why you have this desire in your heart, and it's because you just won't be happy unless you follow your passion no matter what. Playing it safe all the time has never helped someone get an edge over everybody else. If you want to be average, then do what everybody does. If you want to be better, do something different.

Everyone's story is unique. There's no right or wrong, no formula or strategy that works equally well for everyone.

There are all variations of the path someone took to win in life. There are no rules that apply one hundred percent of the time and for everyone's life, no prescriptions, no recipes to follow that guarantee success. Your story is unique. Begin rewriting your own story today and see how it unfolds one day at a time. What will it be? You decide.

What you do today, tomorrow, next week, next month, next year, will determine your future. Sharpening your blade every single day, you will come closer to being the best version of yourself, always improving and learning. It's the many little things that add up and make you the best. It's never luck or one single action.

Even after singing professionally for decades, I still evolve, and my voice keeps changing all the time. I learn new repertoire, try new techniques, understand new concepts, experiment, go through easy and tough times, and continuously look for ways to make singing easier and more efficient, and I constantly work on developing my ear and musical skills.

My voice is different every day and I learn to deal with these differences. I figure out what affects my voice positively or negatively, how my psyche influences my performance as well as my body, and I make better lifestyle choices that help my body perform at its best.

Voices are as diverse as life itself, and it's a miracle to see all of life's facets evolve throughout our lives. Open your eyes, so you become more conscious of this miracle of life. It's a proven fact that even our genes can be turned on or off throughout our lives so that we can even influence our DNA by our behavior and lifestyle choices. The field of epigenetics is fascinating and can give anyone hope that - even though a lot of things in life may be predetermined by your genetics -

you can still shape your own life by turning some genes on or off.

Don't let the constant ups and downs of life frustrate you. Instead, let it be a fascinating journey that you never want to end. The journey is the destination, and the infinite possibilities of expressing your feelings in a new way every day will never allow any boredom. True excellence is created when you gain access to the divine miracles of expressing your soul with your genuinely amazing physical body in a way that unites your spirit with the essence of life. Being vulnerable yet confident, being genuine yet artistic is the essence of a great singer and our humanness.

Your mindset is one of the major determining factors in how your story will continue. Research shows that the most successful people in history didn't become successful by having mere talent, but much rather by putting in a lot of work to become the master of their craft and by just being gritty. Progress isn't made by leaps and bounds, but by hammering away little by little every single day until you have sculpted your skills into precisely what you want them to be.

You know the saying that every journey begins with the first step. Well, while this is true, you will not get far by just taking the first step and then taking a long break or even quitting because you didn't reach your destination yet. Taking the next step, and then the next one, and the next one and next one, until you reach your destination - no matter how tedious, exhausting, or scary that next step may, will inevitably bring you closer and closer to your goals. Will there be disappointments? Absolutely! Will there be defeat? For sure! Will you want to give up sometimes? You bet! But each time doubt creeps in, just tell yourself to take one more step, and after that one just one more, and after that just another one. And before you know it, you will have run a full marathon.

Every seemingly overnight success story has a story leading up to that success. You often don't know what came before, but those success stories that last always had a marathon that preceded the moment of fame.

Yes, it takes training to build endurance, and that's exactly what you're doing by taking just the next step. You will get better every day, and what used to feel hard will get easier. There will be new obstacles all the time, but after a while, you learn to turn the obstacles into wins, because they make you stronger. If you only run a straight road, you won't get as strong as when you run up and downhill. Your muscles will have to work a lot harder, always adjusting to new conditions. After a while, there are just a bunch of recurring patterns you recognize and can handle easily. In music, this is very much the case. Once you have the basic principles down, everything else is just a variation of those principles. Your brain will automatically know what drawer to pull to sing that phrase because some variation has occurred before.

It's like a language: in the beginning, it's tough to learn a new language, since you're not familiar with the structures yet. Even small children still make a lot of mistakes when it comes to grammar and articulation. But as they grow older and learn the concepts of how to shape all of the sounds with their tongue, lips, teeth, and throat, and also learn what order to put the words in, which personal pronouns to use when, and all the ins and outs of correct grammar, they don't even have to think about it anymore. It all becomes second nature, and even though you may speak a sentence that you've never spoken out before, it always consists of elements you're familiar with. You're just mixing the various elements differently, but that's very easy once you know all of the concepts by heart. You may read a word you've never read, but it still consists of the letters you've known for a long time.

That's why I think music theory and ear training are an essential part of a singer's education. Becoming a master of your craft and becoming aware of all the possibilities you have in creating sound and silence will open up a whole new and gigantic world in you to be creative.

I get so excited when I hear the success stories of students I've worked with. I already get excited when I listen to a voice for the first time, even with all of its imperfections, since I don't just hear the way the voice sounds now, but I hear the potential and the sound it could have once a few skills are acquired that help with more control, like lifting the soft palate, opening the vowels, finding the best placement for a natural, open, resonant sound, great articulation, and clarity.

Please don't ever give up on your voice. God has given it to you to make sound in this world, and you can use it to do something special.

So, begin today - begin becoming the master of your voice. It's your story.

I look forward to hearing your success story. Please let me know about it by sending an email to success@masteryourvoice.tv.

Now, go off into the world and make some music!

Made in the USA
Columbia, SC
11 September 2020